Giving up on random marketing and implementing a solid strategy for quick company expansion is necessary if you want to create a profitable company

I0436240

THE ONE-PAGE

MARKETING

STRATEGY

ATTRACT NEW CLIENTS, INCREASE REVENUE, AND MAKE YOURSELF STAND OUT

THE ONE-PAGE MARKETING STRATEGY

ATTRACT NEW CLIENTS, INCREASE REVENUE, AND MAKE YOURSELF STAND OUT

PUBLISHER'S NOTE

The One-Page Marketing Strategy

Cover By Santo K. Hadden.

Edited by Robert Wallace

Contents

Acknowledgments

I wish I could claim to be some kind of marketing and business whiz and that all the concepts in this book are original to me. To be honest, I gather lovely ideas, but I don't really create anything very often, and when I do, it's usually not interesting enough to write about.

Mal Emery, one of my first business mentors, used to often remark, "I've never had an original idea in my life—it's just too bloody dangerous." Nevertheless, he was and still is a very prosperous businessman and marketer. The key to his success —and mine afterward—was to stop attempting to reinvent the wheel and instead merely imitate things that were shown to work.

It takes a genius to reinvent the wheel, and even then, there's a good chance it won't work out. Since I'm not a genius and detest failure, I would much rather carefully mimic the strategies used by successful people—at least until I've mastered the fundamentals. This increases my chances of success and tips the scales in my favor.

Although I developed the technique that is now known as the 1-Page Marketing Plan (1PMP), many of the ideas and innovations behind successful direct response marketing are credited to other outstanding marketers and company executives.

I may be flattering myself, but I've kept in mind Pablo Picasso's dictum, "Good artists copy; great artists steal," which Steve Jobs often said and which I surely had in mind while compiling these exquisite ideas for this book over the years. Whether or not you think of me as a "great"

I want you to profit from the wealth of tried-and-true business-building concepts that follow, whether you're an "artist" or a crook.

Of course, there is a place for ingenuity and innovation, but in my view, these should come after you have mastered the fundamentals. Many of those fundamentals are covered in this book. While some are based on my own experiences, the majority are from "giants" in my professional life who I have stood on. In no specific sequence, I would like to thank:

Mal Emery Dean Jackson Joe Polish, Pete Godfrey Dan Kennedy

Schramko James Jim Rohn

Frank Kern Godin, Seth

I have received mentorship from a few people directly and from others via books and other works they have created. Whenever I believe that one of them is the source of a concept I'm presenting in this book, I make an effort to give them credit in the footnotes. I'm certain, however, that I have overlooked some individuals or failed to give due credit to their ideas. When you gather ideas over a long period, it may sometimes become difficult to pinpoint their source. I'm sorry for it.

Rather than being a novel marketing idea or concept, the 1-Page Marketing Plan is a breakthrough in execution. It's by far the simplest method available for small businesses to go from having no marketing experience to developing and executing an advanced direct-response marketing strategy. The proposal is reduced to a single page.

Enjoy the concepts in this book and, most importantly, put them into practice in your company. Recall that ignorance is the same as knowing and doing nothing.

INTRODUCTION

What's the deal with this?

The shortest route to the money, if I were to sum up this book in one phrase, would be it. To avoid wasting your time, I have intentionally placed this as early in the book as possible.

This opening statement will undoubtedly turn off a lot of people, and to be honest, I'd much rather they read someone else's business book full of ear-tickling platitudes like "work hard," "follow your passion," "hire the right people," and so on.

Look it up on Amazon if that's what you're looking for. You may find a plethora of business books covering many fluffy ideas and more, most authored by experienced writers and researchers who haven't developed a fast-growing company.

The overt and obvious message of this book is to build your company quickly and enjoy the benefits of that type of success.

It's really bad to run out of oxygen.

According to the well-known quote by Zig Ziglar, "Money isn't everything, but it ranks right up there with oxygen."

Indeed, nothing—absolutely nothing—kills a firm more quickly than a shortage of "oxygen" (money).

Why am I so shamelessly obsessed with making money? There are a few valid explanations.

First of all, almost no company issue can't be resolved with additional funding. It is helpful since almost every company I know has issues. Most of the problems that make running a company difficult can be solved with money.

Second, you have an opportunity to assist others once you have taken care of yourself.

You're lying or you have a pastime rather than a company if you didn't get into business to generate money. Furthermore, although I understand the importance of adding value and improving the world, how much of it will you be able to do if you're broke? Can you assist how many people?

An airline attendant will unavoidably say something along the lines of this when you board and they are going through all the safety procedures: oxygen masks will drop down from above your seat if there is a rapid loss of pressure in the cabin. Put the mask on over your nose and mouth, then tighten the strap. Make sure your mask is on before assisting others if you are traveling with kids or someone who needs assistance.

Before assisting others, why not put on your mask? Because, in addition to being unable to assist anyone else, if you're hunched over your seat from a lack of oxygen, we will soon have to utilize our limited resources to rescue you, or else you will soon pass away.

Being Aware of What to Do

Anthony Greenbank wrote this in The Book of Survival:

You don't need to be an Einstein, have the strength of Hercules, or have the reflexes of a Grand Prix driver to survive an impossible circumstance. All you have to do is know what to do.

The precise proportion of enterprises that fail in their first five years is not often consistent in the data. As much as 90% is estimated by some. That being said, I have never heard this percentage reported as being any lower than 50%. This implies that assuming extreme optimism, there is a 50% probability that you will still be in business in five years.

But here is when things turn nasty. Only companies that stop trade are included in the statistics. They neglect to consider firms that eventually reach a low point and gradually murder their owners or make their lives miserable.

Ever ponder why the majority of small enterprises reach a mediocre plateau?

Pete the plumber, who works sixteen-hour days, weekends, and no vacations and barely makes enough money to live, is at one extreme of the scale. Joe, who employs twenty plumbers in his plumbing firm, is at the other extreme of the spectrum. It seems that calculating the enormous quantities of money that keep coming in is his main line of work.

Small companies sometimes never expand beyond the point at which they produce just enough money to allow the owner or owners to live comfortably. It seems that the owner's attempts to advance only result in frustration, regardless of how hard they try. One of two things may occur at this moment.

They either lose hope in their venture or just accept that it will always be low-paying self-made employment.

Many entrepreneurs would probably be better off simply getting employment in their field. In comparison to the prison they have built for themselves, they would probably work fewer hours, experience less stress, enjoy more benefits, and have more vacation time. Conversely, other entrepreneurs seem to be living their dream lives. They put in decent hours, have a great cash flow from their business, and see steady development. A lot of failing company owners throw the blame on their sector. Certain businesses are indeed struggling; bookstores and video rental companies instantly spring to mind as examples. It may be time to stop losing money and move on if you work in one of these failing or dead sectors, rather than financially torturing yourself to death. This might be especially challenging if you've worked in the field for a long time.

But most of the time, individuals are only playing the blame game when they point the finger at their industry. I often hear the following concerns about the industry: It's overly competitive. There are not enough margins. Online bargain hunters are driving away clients. Nowadays, advertising is ineffective.

But in reality, the industry is seldom at fault since successful people may be found in the same field as you. Naturally, what are they doing differently? is the obvious question.

A lot of small company owners fall into the trap that is detailed in The E-Myth Revisited, a famous book by Michael Gerber. In other words, they are skilled technicians who work in many fields such as plumbing, hair styling, dentistry, and so on. They experience what Gerber refers to as "seizures of entrepreneurship," asking themselves, "Why should I work for this fool employer of mine? Since I'm skilled at what I do, I'll launch my own company.

One of the biggest errors that the majority of small-business entrepreneurs make is this. They move from being employed by a stupid employer to becoming their stupid boss! The important thing to remember is that being proficient in a technical area does not automatically translate into commercial acumen.

Returning to our earlier example, a skilled plumber isn't always the best candidate to lead a plumbing company. It is crucial to recognize this difference since it plays a major role in the failure of the majority of small enterprises. Even if the company's owner is a highly skilled technical expert, his lack of commercial acumen is what makes his enterprise fail.

This is not intended to dissuade individuals from launching their own companies. But you also have to commit to improving not only your technical skills but also your business acumen. A business may be a fantastic means of reaching both financial independence and personal satisfaction, but only for those who can distinguish between the two and know what it takes to manage a successful company.

You're at the right place at the right time if you're skilled in the technical aspect of your work but believe you could use some assistance with the commercial end. This book's main goal is to help you go from uncertainty to clarity so that you will know precisely what to do to succeed in business.

Experts Have Schedules

My favorite television program as a child was The A-Team. I'll give you a synopsis of 99% of the episodes in case you haven't seen them:

1. Adversarial men intimidate and harass a gathering of innocent people.

2. The innocent individual or group implores the A-Team to assist them.

3. The A-Team, a disorganized group of former warriors, battles, degrades and chases the adversaries away.

Every episode would conclude with Hannibal, the A-Team's brains, saying gleefully, "I love it when a plan comes together," while nibbling on his cigar.

Any profession where there are significant risks will have a well-thought-out strategy in place. Professionals never just wing it. Physicians adhere to a therapeutic strategy. Pilots on airlines adhere to a flight plan. Troops adhere to a military operating schedule.

If a member of the aforementioned profession told you to "screw the plan," how would you feel about using their services? I'll just wing it. However, the majority of company owners operate in this manner.

A person's lack of planning is usually evident in the aftermath when they make a mess of something. Keep it from happening to you or your company. Having a strategy greatly raises your chances of success, even if no one can promise it.

You and your family shouldn't be dependent on a company for which you haven't bothered with a business plan, just as you wouldn't want to be on an aircraft if the pilot hadn't bothered with a flight plan. The stakes are often almost as great. Sickness and failure in business sometimes result in the loss of marriages, relationships, careers, and more.

It's time to "go pro" and make a strategy since more than just your ego is at stake.

The Wrong Sort of Scheme

I had the foresight to realize early on in my first company that a business strategy would be critical to its success. Sadly, it was the extent of my intelligence.

I ended up thousands of dollars poorer, but with a document most company owners never bother with—a business plan—thanks to the assistance of a business consultant (who'd never really run a successful firm of his own).

My business strategy was several hundred pages long. It had projections, charts, graphs, and a ton of other stuff. Although it looked amazing, the document was just a collection of meaningless words.

I wrote it, stuffed it in my desk's top drawer, and didn't see it again until the day I had to clear up my desk since we were changing offices.

I threw it in the garbage, skimmed through it, and brushed it off, feeling guilty about wasting so much money on that fake consultant.

But after giving it some more consideration, I saw that even though the paper was full of gibberish, the process I went through with the consultant helped me to understand certain important aspects of my firm, especially one piece that was crucial and was referred to as "the marketing plan."

The work we put into developing the marketing strategy helped to mold the company and pave the way for much of our future success.

I'll talk more about this later, but for now, allow me to introduce you to a guy and his idea that might be the secret to your company's success.

Vilfredo Pareto, my friend, and the 80/20 Rule

Vilfredo Pareto passed away more than 50 years before I was born, so I never had the chance to meet him, but I'm sure we would have been lifelong friends.

Italian economist Pareto observed that 20% of the country's people held 80% of the country's land. Thus, the Pareto Principle —also referred to as the 80/20 rule—was established.

It turns out that there are more applications of the 80/20 rule in Italy than simply property ownership. It applies to practically everything you can imagine. A few instances are: Twenty percent of a company's clients account for 80% of its earnings. Twenty percent of drivers are responsible for 80% of traffic accidents. 20% of users utilize 80% of the program. 20% of a company's consumers account for 80% of its complaints. Twenty percent of individuals hold 80% of the wealth. Even Woody Allen said that putting in the work is 80% of achievement.

Stated differently, the Pareto Principle states that 20% of causes account for 80% of effects.

Perhaps it's just my idleness speaking, but this excites me a lot.

Though it's often believed that need inspires creation, I contend that idleness does, and my buddy Vilfredo is my guide in this endeavor.

In other words, you can get most of the same benefits even if you stop doing 80% of the things you're doing and spend your day eating nachos on the sofa.

Your fastest route to success is to focus more on the 20% of activities if you don't want to spend 80% of your time eating nachos while lounging on the sofa. And success in this case means making more money with less effort.

64/4 Rule

The 64/4 rule will astound you if you find the 80/20 rule intriguing. As you can see, the rule itself is subject to the 80/20 rule. Thus, the 64/4 rule is obtained by taking 80% of 80 and 20% of 20.

Thus, 4% of causes account for 64% of effects.

Put another way, the bulk of your success comes from the top 4% of your acts. To put it another way, 96% of the things you do are (relatively) time-wasting.

The 80/20 rule and 64/4 rule still hold up pretty well, which is the most astonishing thing. Statistics on wealth distribution over the last century show that the top 4% hold over 64% of the total wealth, while the top 20% control almost 80% of it. This is true even if we live in the "information age." It seems logical that only the rich would have had excellent access to knowledge a century ago, which explains why they had 80% of the wealth.

Even in this day of information democratization, when even the poorest individuals have almost equal access to knowledge as the richest, this wealth distribution figure remains valid.

This demonstrates that human behavior and mentality, not a lack of knowledge, are the things preventing the bottom 80% of company owners from succeeding. That hasn't altered in the last century, for sure.

The Rich People's Best Kept Secret

One factor sets apart the extraordinarily successful and affluent company owners from the struggling and bankrupt ones, based on my observations of and interactions with various business owners worldwide.

While prosperous company owners will spend money to save time, struggling business owners will spend time to save money. Why is that difference significant? Because you can always get more money, but you can never get more time. Therefore, you must make sure that the things you focus on have the most potential effect.

Leverage is what we call this, and it's the wealthiest people's best-hidden secret.

The pivotal 20% of the 80/20 rule and the 4% of the 64/4 rule are made up of these significant, leveraged operations.

You have to start focusing on and growing in the areas where you have the most leverage if you want to be more successful.

There are many places in your company where you might begin searching for sources of leverage. You may consider improving your negotiating abilities by 50%. As a result, you may be able to renegotiate with important suppliers and get a little increase in your purchase price. Even though this is fantastic, after all that time and work, your bottom line has just slightly increased. I wouldn't classify this as having enormous leverage. Not gradual, but exponential progress is what we want.

Marketing is by far the most powerful tool in any company. Your bottom line may increase exponentially or double if you improve your marketing skills by 10%.

American bank robber Willie Sutton was a prolific thief. He stole millions of dollars during his forty-year criminal career, ended up serving more than half of his adult life in jail, and made three successful escapes. Reporter Mitch Ohnstad questioned Sutton about his motivations for robbing banks.

He said, "Because that's where the money is," according to Ohnstad. The same logic applies to business, where we want to place a strong emphasis on marketing since that's where the money is.

Utilizing the 64/4 and 80/20 Rules in Your Marketing Strategy

Rewind to my last tale about the incorrect kind of company strategy. Making the marketing strategy was the one aspect of the business planning process that paid off for me, even if my business plan paper turned out to be a meaningless jumble of management speak and gibberish.

In the end, the marketing strategy accounted for 20% of the total outcome of the business planning process.

Since then, this has been the situation in every company I've founded and operated.

Having this in mind, I made it a major goal when I began advising small company owners to develop marketing plans.

What do you think? Not many of them ever followed through on it. Why? Because developing a marketing strategy required much work and was something that most small company owners would never accomplish.

Thus, once again, indolence turns into the source of creativity.

I had to find a method to distill the essential elements of the marketing planning process into something small company owners could easily understand and use. The 1-page Marketing Plan was born.

The 1-page marketing plan represents the 4% of work that yields 64% (or higher) of the desired outcome for your company. Applying the 64/4 rule to company planning is what it is. By using this method, we can reduce conventional business planning's hundreds of pages and thousands of hours to a single page that only requires 30 minutes to think about and complete.

Even more fascinating is that it becomes a live record in your company. One that you can hang on your workplace wall, consult, and improve with time. Above all, it's useful. There's no confusing jargon or managerial speak. To build it or comprehend it, you don't need an MBA.

One of the biggest innovations in marketing execution is the one-page marketing plan. I've seen a noticeable increase in coaching clients' compliance rates. Small company owners now have access to conventional marketing plans, even if they would never have had the time, resources, or expertise to do so. They have so enjoyed the enormous advantages that come with having clarity in their marketing.

I'll soon provide the one-page marketing plan, but for now, I believe it would be best to start from scratch and make no assumptions. Even so-called professionals and industry specialists find it difficult to understand the phrase "marketing."

Let's take a moment to quickly review the definition of marketing.

Marketing: What Is It?

Some individuals believe that marketing is just branding, advertising, or some other nebulous idea. Even though they are

THE ONE-PAGE MARKETING STRATEGY

all related to marketing, they are not the same thing.

This is the clearest, most basic explanation of marketing you'll ever find:

It is advertising if you paint a sign that reads, "Circus Coming to the Showground Saturday," in advance of the circus's arrival in your community.

Promotion is when you take an elephant into town with a sign attached to its back.

Publicity occurs when an elephant strolls past the mayor's flower garden and is reported in the local newspaper.

And if you get the mayor to chuckle about it, that's public relations.

If the residents of the town visit the circus, you tour them around the various entertainment booths, tell them how much fun they will have spending money at the booths, respond to their inquiries, and eventually they wind up spending a lot of money there, which is what's known as sales.

And that's marketing if you plan the whole thing.

Yes, that's right, marketing is the tactic you use to make your ideal target market aware of you, like you, and have enough faith in you to become a client. Everything you often think of as marketing is a technique. We'll go into strategy vs. tactics in greater detail shortly.

But before we do that, you must realize that things have changed fundamentally over the last ten years, and they will never return to how they were.

The Responses Have Been Modified

There was a day when Albert Einstein gave his graduating class an exam paper. It came out that he had given them the same test paper the year before. Einstein was informed by his teaching assistant, who was disturbed by what he witnessed and believed it to be the consequence of the professor's inattention.

"Pardon me, sir," the bashful assistant murmured, unsure of how to break the news to the great man about his error.

Yes, Einstein replied.

"It's about the test you just gave out, um." Einstein bided his time.

"This is the same exam you administered last year; I'm not sure whether you recognize that. It is, in actuality, the same.

After pausing briefly to gather his thoughts, Einstein said, "Yes, the test is the same, but the answers have changed."

The answers in business and marketing are subject to change in tandem with discoveries, just like the answers in physics.

Once upon a time, you paid a hefty fee to publish an advertisement in the Yellow Pages, and your year's worth of marketing was complete. Google, social media, blogs, websites, and a plethora of additional considerations are now on your plate.

There are a ton of competitors now that the Internet exists. Your competition can suddenly be on the other side of the world from where they used to be across the street.

This causes the "bright shiny object syndrome" to paralyze many people attempting to sell their firm. Here's where they come into

engrossed in whatever "hot" marketing strategies are popular at the moment, such as SEO, video, podcasting, pay-per-click advertising, and so on.

They get mired in methods and instruments and fail to see the larger picture of their true goals and motivations.

Allow me to demonstrate why this will result in immense suffering.

Pitching versus scheming

The secret to successful marketing is knowing the difference between strategy and tactics.

The broad preparation you conduct before implementing the methods is called strategy. Assume you want to construct a home on an empty plot of land that you have purchased. Would you just place an order for a bunch of bricks and begin placing them? Naturally, no. You would be left with a massive, probably unsafe mess.

What do you do in its place now? First, you employ an architect and a builder, and they handle all the planning, from obtaining construction licenses to selecting the kind of tap fittings you want. This is all planned out before a single shovel of soil is lifted. That's the plan.

After you have a plan in place, you can determine how many bricks you'll need, where to put the foundation, and what style of roof you want. You may now engage carpenters, electricians, plumbers, bricklayers, and so on. That's a strategy.

You cannot effectively do anything of value without both strategy and tactics.

Without tactics, strategy becomes paralyzed by analysis. The home will never be constructed, no matter how skilled the architect and builder are, unless bricks are laid. They will eventually have to declare, "All right, the blueprint is now sound. Let's begin building—we have all the required permissions in place.

The "bright, shiny object syndrome" results from using tactics without a plan. Consider the following scenario: You begin constructing a wall without any blueprints, discover later that it is not the proper location, pour the foundation, and discover later that it is not appropriate for this kind of home. You then begin digging the area where you want the pool, only to discover that it is also incorrect. This will not work. However, many company owners do their marketing in this manner.

They combine several haphazard strategies in the hopes that one of them will result in a client. They throw together a hastily constructed website that becomes an online brochure, or they begin marketing on social media because they've heard it's the newest thing, and so on.

To succeed, you need both strategy and tactics, but your plan must come first as it determines the techniques you employ. Here's where your marketing strategy comes into play: Consider your marketing strategy as the building block used by the architect to attract and keep clients.

Do I Need Marketing If I Have a Great Product or Service?

Many entrepreneurs delude themselves into believing that if their product is superior, customers will come. The idea that "if you build it, they will come" is a horrible business plan, but it makes for a fantastic movie narrative. This is a costly approach that has a high failure rate. Technically excellent goods that were not successful economically are numerous throughout history. Examples include, but are not limited to, Betamax, Newton, and LaserDisc.

Simply put, excellent goods are insufficient. One of your main priorities if you want your firm to succeed should be marketing.

Consider this: When does a potential customer learn how excellent your item or service is? When they purchase is, of course, the response. They won't know how wonderful your goods or services are if they don't purchase from you. As the renowned IBM employee Thomas Watson once said, "Nothing happens until a sale is made."

Thus, we must comprehend this key idea: a quality product or service serves as a tool for retaining customers. If we provide our consumers with an excellent product or service, they will return for future purchases, recommend us to others, and help to strengthen the brand via good word-of-mouth. But first, we must consider client acquisition (often known as marketing) before customer retention. The most successful businesspeople usually begin with marketing.

How to End Your Company

In the sincere hope that you won't do it, I'm going to share with you one of the simplest and most frequent methods to destroy your company. It's without a doubt the top marketing error committed by small-business entrepreneurs.

This is a common issue that is the main cause of the majority of small company marketing failures.

It is quite likely that small company owners have considered marketing and advertising. Which strategy are you planning to employ? What will you say in your marketing campaign?

Small-business entrepreneurs often make this decision by observing their successful, well-established rivals in their sector and adopting their strategies. It makes sense to follow the lead of other prosperous companies to achieve success yourself. Correct?

This is indeed the quickest path to failure, and I do not doubt that it accounts for the majority of small company failures. These are the two main causes of this.

#1: Big Businesses Have Different Goals

When it comes to marketing, large corporations have quite different goals than small enterprises. Their techniques and priorities vary greatly from yours.

A significant company's marketing objectives may resemble this:

1. Appeasing the directors' board

2. Fulfilling the needs of shareholders

3. Easing the prejudices of superiors

4. Fulfilling the expectations of the current clientele

5. Obtaining creative and advertising accolades

6. Obtaining support from different committees and interested parties

7. Turning a profit

A small company owner's top marketing priority may resemble this:

1. Turning a profit

As you can see, small and big businesses have quite different marketing objectives. Therefore, it would stand to reason that strategy and execution would vary greatly.

#2: Large companies have a very different budget. Strategy varies with size. You must comprehend this. Do you believe that the typical modest property owner has a different approach to real estate investing than someone who invests in and builds skyscrapers? Of course.

On a small scale, the same approach is just not going to be effective. Building a single-story skyscraper is not enough to achieve success. All 100 stories are required.

If you have a $10 million advertising budget and three years to turn a profit, you would use a very different approach than someone who just has a $10,000 budget and has to turn a profit right now.

When compared to a huge company's marketing approach, $10,000 won't go very far. The reason it will be completely useless and wasteful is because the technique you are implementing is inappropriate for the size at which you are operating.

Big Business Promotion

Mass marketing or "branding" are other terms used to describe large-scale corporate marketing. Reminding clients and prospects of your brand and the goods and services you provide is the aim of this kind of advertising.

The theory behind this is that the more often you advertise your brand, the more probable it is that consumers will think of it first when they are ready to make a purchase.

This encompasses the bulk of marketing initiatives for huge corporations. You've probably seen advertisements for well-known companies like Apple, Nike, and Coca-Cola.

Although this kind of marketing works well, it requires a lot of time and money to execute well. It calls for you to heavily and consistently advertise across a range of platforms, including print, radio, television, and the internet.

The big businesses don't mind the cost or time commitment since they have large advertising budgets, teams of marketers, and product lines that are planned years in advance.

However, when small firms attempt to use this kind of marketing to mimic large brands, a serious issue occurs.

Their rare ad runs are like a drop in the ocean. With hundreds of marketing messages reaching their target market every day, it is by no means sufficient to get beyond the threshold of awareness. As a result, they are overwhelmed and get little to no return on their investment. Another victim of advertising goes down in flames.

It's not like major media advertisements or "branding" aren't effective for small firms. The issue is that they just lack the funding to broadcast their advertisements often enough to be successful.

You have a very high chance of failing with this kind of marketing unless you have millions of dollars allocated to it.

Big businesses are the ones that handle branding, mass marketing, and ego-based marketing. Utilizing pricey mass media and a large budget is necessary to accomplish any form of cut-through.

It's wise to follow in the footsteps of previous successful companies, but you must be able to carry out and fully comprehend the approach you're implementing.

From the viewpoint of an outsider, strategy might vary significantly from reality. It is quite improbable that a plan you are adopting that differs much in terms of money or priorities from your own would provide the type of outcome you are aiming for.

Let's now examine the elements of a good small- to medium-sized company marketing strategy.

Marketing for Small and Medium-Sized Businesses

One specific area of marketing that helps small companies stand out and get a competitive advantage on a tight budget is direct response marketing. It is intended to guarantee that you get a quantifiable return on your investment.

How many $10 notes would you purchase if they were being offered for $2 each? Naturally, as many as you can get your hands on! "Money at a discount" is the name of the game in direct response marketing. For instance, you get $10 in sales revenue for every $2 you spend on advertising.

It's also a moral kind of marketing. It is targeted at the particular issues that the prospect has and seeks to address them with targeted education and remedies. It's also the only practical option for a small firm to contact a potential customer at a reasonable price.

Your advertising becomes lead-generating tools instead of merely name-recognition ones when you convert them to direct-response ads.

The goal of direct response marketing is to get a reaction right away and force potential customers to do a certain action, such as signing up for your email list, giving you a call to get more information, making an order, or visiting a website. What then constitutes a direct-response advertisement? Here are a few of the salient features:

It can be tracked. In other words, you can determine which advertisement and which media outlet sparked a reaction when someone did. Unlike mass media or "brand" marketing, which you may not even be aware of, no one will ever know what advertisement made you purchase Coke.

It can be measured. You can determine the precise effectiveness of each advertisement as you are aware of which ones are generating responses and how many sales they have generated. The advertising that isn't providing you with a return on investment is then changed or dropped.

Sales copy and attention-grabbing headlines are used. The persuasive message of direct response marketing will pique the attention of your targeted prospects. It employs compelling headlines and persuasive sales language, or "salesmanship in print." The advertisement often resembles an editorial rather than a commercial, increasing its likelihood of being read at least three times.

It caters to a particular market or specialty. Targeted prospects are those in certain verticals, regions, or niche markets. A specific target market is the focus of the advertisement.

It presents a precise proposal. Ads often provide a targeted, highly valuable offer. Getting the prospect to click through to the next step, such as requesting a free report, is often the goal rather than making a sale from the advertisement. The offer discusses the prospect's interests, wants, worries, and frustrations while putting the prospect front and center rather than the marketer. Mass media, or "brand," marketing, on the other hand, focuses on the advertiser and has a wide, one-size-fits-all message.

It needs an answer. A "call to action" appears in direct response advertising, urging the potential customer to take a certain action. It also has a way to react and "capture" these reactions. There are many simple methods to get in touch with interested, high-probability prospects: a standard phone number, a free recorded message line, a website, a fax-back form, a reply card, or coupons. To stay in touch with the prospect after they have responded, as much of their contact information as possible is recorded when they reply.

It consists of many steps and a quick follow-up. Important education and information on the prospect's issue are provided in return for gathering the prospect's data. A second "irresistible offer" should be included with the material, linked to whatever action you would want the prospect to take next, such as giving you a call to make an appointment or visiting the shop or showroom. Subsequently, a sequence of more "touches" via other mediums, including mail,

Phone, fax, and email are sent. Frequently, an offer has a time or quantity restriction.

It includes maintenance follow-up for leads that are not converted. There might be a variety of reasons why a potential customer does not "mature" into a sale right away if they do not reply within the brief follow-up time. This bank of slow-maturing possibilities has worth. They ought to be cared for and should still get frequent updates from you.

The issue of direct response marketing is complex and

multifaceted. You don't have to spend years studying to become an expert in direct response marketing to use it in your organization with the aid of the 1-Page Marketing Plan.

It's a guided approach that makes it simple and fast to put together the essential components of a direct response campaign for your company.

The One-Page Marketing Strategy

The purpose of the 1-Page Marketing Strategy (1PMP) canvas is to allow you to complete it in point form as you read this book, resulting in a customized marketing strategy for your company. This is the appearance of a blank 1PMP canvas:

There are nine squares broken up into the three primary stages of the marketing process. Good marketing, like most great plays, movies, and novels, is organized into three acts. Let us examine these three "acts."

The Marketing Journey's Three Phases

We aim to lead our ideal target market through the marketing process. Our goal is to lead them from being unaware of our existence to becoming devoted customers.

We accompany them through three different stages of their adventure. These stages correspond to your marketing process's before, during, and after phases. Here's a quick rundown of each of these stages:

Before

Prospects are those who are going through the previous phase. In the early stages of the "before" phase, most prospects are unaware of your existence. When this step is finished well, the prospect expresses interest and knows who you are.

For instance, Tom, a busy company owner, is annoyed when his contacts don't sync between his smartphone and laptop. In his quest for a solution, he stumbles into an advertisement titled "Five Little-Known Strategies That Unlock the Power of Your

Business IT System" online. After clicking on the advertisement, Tom is sent to an online form where he has to provide his email address to get a complimentary report. Tom inputs his email address because he thinks the report has something valuable to share.

During

Those who are in the period are referred to as leads. The "during" phase has begun, and leads have shown some interest in your offer. The successful completion of this step leads to the prospect purchasing from you for the first time.

Example: Tom finds the report he downloaded to be very valuable. He didn't know any of its very excellent advice before, and putting it into practice has saved him a ton of time. Furthermore, Tom has been receiving emails from the IT firm that created the report with further helpful advice and information, along with an offer for a free 21-point IT assessment for his company. Tom accepts their invitation. Tom learns from the meticulous and expert audit that many of the programs on his PCs are outdated, which puts his IT systems at risk. Furthermore, six months ago, the backups he believed to be occurring ceased functioning. They offer to send a technician at a much-reduced cost to remedy any issues found during the audit. Tom accepts their invitation.

Following

At this stage, we refer to individuals as customers. 3. The "after" phase starts with clients having previously paid you money. The after phase never stops and, when done well, creates a positive feedback loop where the consumer keeps coming back to you and becomes so enamored with your offerings that they constantly refer you to others and bring you in new business.

Example: Tom is very pleased with the technician's professionalism in resolving his IT issues. The technician was polite, on time, and gave Tom a clear explanation of everything.

Crucially, he keeps his company's pledge of "Fixed First Time or It's Free." The next day, a representative from headquarters contacts Tom to find out whether he is happy with the assistance he got. Tom gives the impression that he is very happy. On this follow-up contact, Tom is presented with a maintenance plan that includes fixed monthly maintenance for his IT systems, performed by a certified specialist. Additionally, it comes with limitless technical support, so Tom can contact a toll-free number at any moment and receive prompt assistance if he gets stuck. Tom accepts this invitation. He routinely wastes productive time trying to find out how to repair his IT system; thus, the helpline alone is valuable to him. Tom even sends three of his business buddies from his golf club to this organization because of the outstanding service he's encountered.

In conclusion, the three stages might look somewhat like this if we were to list them in a table:

Phase Objective: This Phase

Before ProspectLead: Make them like you and make their first purchase. Get them to know you and show interest.

Following CustomerGain their trust so they will continue to purchase from you and recommend you to others.

Now that we have a clear picture of the general layout, it is time to examine each of the nine squares that comprise your one-page marketing plan in more detail.

ACT I: THE PRELIMINARY STAGE

CHAPTER 1: CHOOSING YOUR IDEAL CUSTOMER

CHOOSING YOUR IDEAL CUSTOMER

Many company owners say "everyone" when I ask them who their target customer is. This indicates that nobody. Many entrepreneurs want to service as large a market as they can in their rush to attract as many clients as they can.

This seems sensible on the surface. However, this is a tremendous error. Being cautious not to leave out any possible clients is a common concern among entrepreneurs when it comes to limiting their target market.

This is a common error made by novice marketers. We'll look at why turning away clients is beneficial in this chapter.

The majority of big business advertising, as covered in the Introduction, belongs to a kind of advertising known as mass marketing, which is also sometimes termed "branding." When using this kind of marketing, company owners are like archers in a thick fog, aiming their arrows in all directions and hoping that one or more of them will strike the goal.

The idea behind mass marketing is that you want to "make your brand known." I'm not entirely clear what should happen when your name gets "there" or where "there" is. In any case, the idea is that if you broadcast your message often enough, you may just happen to reach a potential audience, and a portion of them will become customers.

You would be correct if it sounds a lot like our lost archer, stumbling about in the mist, aiming his arrows in all directions, and crossing his fingers. But you may be wondering, what if he simply fires enough arrows?

In every direction, he will undoubtedly reach his objective. Correct? Perhaps, but that's a dumb marketing strategy for small- to medium-sized enterprises at least, since they'll never have enough arrows—that is, money—to strike their target often enough to get a fair return on their investment.

A laser-like concentration on a certain target market, commonly referred to as a niche, is essential for small company marketing success.

Niching: Using Focus to Its Advantage

Let's identify a company specialty first before continuing.

A narrowly defined area within a subcategory is called a niche. Consider the categories of health and beauty, for instance. This category is quite broad. Numerous treatments, such as tanning, waxing, facials, massage, cellulite treatment, and much more, may be provided by a beauty salon. This may be our specialty if we choose one of these subcategories, such as cellulite therapy. Nonetheless, we may concentrate on treating cellulite in women who have just given birth to further narrow it down. This is a very specific niche. You could be asking yourself, "Why in the world would we want to limit our market so much?" This is the reason why:

1. The quantity of money you have is restricted. Your marketing message will become weak and diluted if you place too much emphasis on it.

The second important component is relevancy. Your advertisement should make potential customers think, "Hey, that's for me."

Would you be interested in an advertisement that specifically targeted cellulite as a postpartum lady worried about it? Without a doubt, What if the advertisement was a generic one for a beauty parlor that listed a plethora of services, including cellulite treatment? It would probably be overlooked in the chaos.

A room is illuminated by a 100-watt light bulb, similar to the ones we often have in our houses. A 100-watt laser, on the other hand, can cut through steel. Same energy, but a vastly different effect. The way the energy is directed makes a difference. It applies the same principle to your marketing.

Consider one more photographer as an example. Most photographers' advertisements include a long list of services, such as Headshots and family photos Commercial images Fashion shots

Although the technical aspects of photography may not vary much across scenarios, allow me to pose a question to you. Do you believe that a person seeking wedding photos would react differently to an advertisement than someone seeking business photos?

Do you believe that a purchasing manager from a heavy equipment distributor wanting to shoot a truck for a product brochure would have quite different needs than a bride-to-be searching for a photographer for her special day? Of course.

But if the advertisement only presents a long list of services without communicating with any prospects, it is irrelevant and will probably be disregarded by both market groups.

For this reason, you must choose a specific target market for your marketing initiative.

Failure in marketing is the result of trying to please everyone. This does not preclude you from providing a wide variety of services; rather, realize that every service category is its campaign.

It's possible to become a large fish in a tiny pond by focusing on a narrow specialty. It makes it feasible for you to rule a region or category in a manner that is not achievable with generality.

You should target niches that are "an inch wide and a mile deep." An inch wide indicates that it is a narrowly focused subset of a given category. A mile deep indicates that many individuals are searching for a solution to that particular issue. Once you have mastered one niche, you may grow your company by identifying and mastering a second, equally lucrative, and highly focused specialty.

With this, you may still benefit from being highly targeted while expanding the potential scale of your company.

Niching Removes Price's Significance

Which medical professional would you rather see if you had recently had a heart attack—a general practitioner or a cardiac specialist? You would naturally choose the expert. Would you anticipate paying more for a meeting with a cardiac specialist than you would with a general practitioner, then? Of course.

You're not shopping on price; therefore, your bill from the specialist is probably going to be substantially greater than your general practitioner's.

How did pricing become unimportant all of a sudden? The appeal of catering to a niche lies in that. You may now charge significantly more for your services than you could as a generalist, regardless of whether you perform heart surgery or provide cellulite treatment. Your prospects and consumers see you in various ways. Experts are in high demand instead of being bought cheaply. A jack-of-all-trades is not nearly as regarded as a specialist. An expert receives a hefty salary for helping their target market with a particular issue.

Choose the one problem that your target audience is looking for a solution for, and they will gladly pay you for it. Then go to the mental dialogue they are having, ideally one that they worry about before going to bed and continue to think about after waking up. Do this, and your results will substantially improve.

In actuality, aiming for everyone implies aiming for no one. You lose your "specialness" and become a commodity that can be purchased based just on price if you go too far. You become an expert by focusing on a small subset of the market that you can impress and service with exceptional outcomes.

Naturally, you choose who to exclude when you narrow down your target market. Never undervalue the significance of this. A lot of small company owners are afraid of losing out on prospective consumers. They make the error of thinking that a larger net would draw in more clients. This is a tremendous error. Once you've established dominance over a niche, follow suit.

with one more, and then another. But never do so in one go. You lose marketing strength and your message when you do this.

How to Determine Who Your Perfect Client Is

Now that you understand the benefits of selecting a specific target market, it's time to choose your own. You could now cater to several market niches, as is the case with most companies. Returning to our buddy the photographer, he may, for instance, do: marriagesBusiness-related photos Journalistic photography, and family photos

These market sectors are quite different. Using the PVP index 4 (personal satisfaction, value to the marketplace, and profitability) and assigning a score of 10 to each market group you serve is an excellent method to determine your optimal target market.

P: Personal fulfillment: To what extent do you find interacting with this kind of client enjoyable? We sometimes deal with "pain in the butt" clients just for financial gain. You may score your level of enjoyment working with this market segment here.

V: Value to the market: How much is your work valued by this particular market segment? Do they intend to provide you with a high salary for your efforts?

P: Profitability: What is the profitability of your job for this particular market segment? Even with large prices charged, your job may sometimes be barely profitable or even loss-making when you look at the figures. Recall that the "leftover" is what matters most—not the "turnover."

In the case of our photographer, his PVP index may be like this:

marriages

Individual fulfillment = 5. Market value = 7 Profits = 9

21 overallJournalistic Photography

Individual satisfaction = 9 Market value = 7 Earnings = 2

18 overall

Business-related photos family photos

Three personal fulfillments plus six profits from the market equal nine. Individual satisfaction = 9 Market value = 8 Earnings = 9

18 overall 26 overall

Those seeking family photographs are the photographer's dream clients. These are the most enjoyable, lucrative, valuable, and well-paying kinds of clients. You, too, probably belong to a unique market category.

While our marketing efforts will be focused on one ideal market segment for the time being, this does not imply that you cannot accept work from outside of your ideal target market. We want to be laser-focused. We can add other market segments once we have control over this one. Our marketing efforts will be futile if we target a wide range of market groups and are initially too broad.

Who is the perfect consumer base for you? Provide as much detail as you can about any characteristic that could be important. What are their age, gender, and location?

Do you own a photo of them? If so, after you consider and respond to the following questions, cut out or print a picture of them: What causes their dyspepsia to flare up in their esophagus, eyes wide open, as they stare at the ceiling at night? What fears do they harbor? For what reason are they upset? They are upset about whom? What annoys them the most every day? Which trends are they seeing and will they be seeing in their lives or businesses? What is their greatest, most hidden desire? Is their decision-making process inherently biased? Engineers, for instance, are quite analytical. Do they speak in a language or employ jargon unique to themselves? Which periodicals are they reading? Which websites do they browse? How is the day going for this person? What is the primary, prevailing feeling in this market? What is it that they yearn for more than anything else?

These inquiries are neither theoretical nor idealistic. Their performance in marketing is crucial. No matter how skillfully you carry out your other marketing initiatives, they will all be ineffective unless you can get access to your prospect's head.

A significant portion of your first marketing efforts should go into doing in-depth interviews, research, and detailed analysis of your target market unless you are a member of that market.

Make an Avatar

Making an avatar that represents your prospect is one of the finest ways to momentarily enter their head. I won't be all woo-woo on you here, so don't worry.

An avatar is a thorough examination and depiction of your ideal clientele and their lifestyle. You put together a composite, like a police sketch artist, and you obtain a clear mental image of them. It helps in telling their tale so you may picture life from their point of view.

Making avatars for every kind of influencer or decision-maker you could come across in your target market is also crucial. For instance, you could interact with both the firm owners and their helpers if you offer IT services to small financial services organizations.

Here is an example of an avatar for Max Cash, who runs a profitable financial planning business, and Angela Assistant, his assistant.

Maximum CashMax is fifty-one years old. Over the last 10 years, his profitable financial planning firm has expanded rapidly. Before going out on his own, he had a career working for KPMG and a few other major corporations. He has both an MBA and a bachelor's degree. He is married, and he has a younger son and two adolescent daughters. He has been living in a five-bedroom home in an upper-middle-class suburb for almost four years. He has a Mercedes S-Class that is two years old. He works out of an office facility he owns with eighteen employees. He drives fifteen minutes to work from his house. The company brings in $4.5 million a year, the majority of which comes from services. The majority of his IT and tech duties are delegated to his PA, Angela Assistant since he does not employ an IT support worker. He pays around $4,000 a month for the several software programs that his sector uses to acquire the most recent financial data. Although he is aware of the software's benefits to both himself and his customers, he is also aware of how many functionalities are being underutilized. His software providers installed most of the PCs that make up his office server and systems, which have had relatively little maintenance since they were deployed. The backup mechanisms are antiquated and have never been tested. He is an avid golfer. Memorabilia related to golf adorns his workspace. Throughout, there are pictures of him on the golf course. His computer's desktop wallpaper is an exquisite panoramic image of Pebble Beach

Golf Links. Naturally, he enjoys playing golf with his friends and business acquaintances in his free time. He reads his local newspaper, Bloomberg BusinessWeek, and The Wall Street Journal. Although he has an iPhone, he mostly uses it for phone calls and sometimes for email.

May you see how this may provide us with important information about our prospect's life? Let's now examine the avatar of a different influencer in our intended market:

Assistant Angela: At 29 years old, Angela is unmarried and lives with her cat, Sprinkles, in a leased two-bedroom apartment. She travels every day to work using public transportation.

around half an hour. Angela is an extremely motivated, well-groomed, and orderly person. Over the last three years, as the company's development has truly accelerated, Angela has served as Max's PA. Without her, he would be completely lost, since she is his right hand. In addition to setting up Max's phone and laptop and managing his schedule, she also answers and places calls on his behalf. She does a little bit of everything for Max's company, from purchasing stationery to handling HR and IT. She's the glue that keeps it all together. Despite the title "PA," she is more than that. She is the manager of the office and maybe even the general manager to some degree. When anything has to be mended, sorted, or organized, the staff goes to her. Although she is technologically literate, she is completely unprepared for the more complex and strategic aspects of IT systems. She enjoys watching new Netflix series and working out at the gym after work. She enjoys going out to bars and hanging out with friends on the weekends. She reads blogs about fashion, beauty, and celebrity rumors when she's online. The majority of Angela's disposable cash is consumed by her entertainment, dining out, and internet shopping, which she treats like an addiction. Despite receiving a good salary, Angela is always short on cash, which has led to her accruing around $10,000 in credit card debt. She knows she has to be better with money, but there always seem to be too many temptations for her to refuse. She is addicted to her phone, using social media applications, and sending texts nonstop.

To go one step further, choose a real picture to serve as your avatar's visual representation, and always have it in front of you as you create marketing.

content for them.

I hope you can see now how powerful avatars may be. They are method acting's inverse in marketing terms. They provide you direct access to your prospect's head, which is invaluable insight when developing your message for your intended audience.

CHAPTER 2: MESSAGE CRAFTING

MESSAGE CRAFTING

Invest a lot of time searching through local and national media outlets for advertisements rather than articles. With very few exceptions throughout many years, I've been doing this, and I'm always shocked at how dull, repetitive, and pointless most advertising is. The level of trash is astounding. both financial and opportunity waste.

The majority of small company advertisements may be summed up as follows:

Name of the company Business emblem

An extensive list of the services provided

Proclamations of the highest quality, greatest value, or best rates Provision of a "free quote"

Details of contact

It's simply a name, rank, and serial number. Then, they hope and pray that a prospect in urgent need of their product or service will see their advertisement and act on the same day it appears. I refer to this as "marketing by accident." Sometimes a transaction happens by fortunate accident—a qualified prospect happens to see the correct ad at the right moment.

No one would ever advertise if these "accidents" had never occurred. But as it occurs, this kind of promotion may sometimes result in an unexpected lead or sale. It kills company owners by torturing them during the advertisement.

normally costs them money, but they dread stopping running it since some dribs and drabs of new business have come out of it —and who knows, next week it may bring in the big sale they've been looking for.

These companies seem to be playing a slot machine at a casino. They insert their funds, turn the handle, and hold out hope for a big win, but the house often simply takes their money. Sometimes they may get a few cents back on a dollar, which gives them hope and confidence to keep going.

It's time to start promoting with intention; approach advertising not like a slot machine where the chances are stacked against you and the outcomes are unpredictable, but like a vending machine where the value created and results are predictable.

To begin marketing intentionally, we must consider two essential components:

1. What is the advertisement's goal?

2. What is the main focus of your advertisement?

Usually, when I ask company owners what their advertisement's goal is, they give me a list like this: branding Putting my name out there promoting my goods and services to others. generating revenue Persuading consumers to get quotes via phone

As each of them is so unique, it is not possible to complete them all with a single advertisement. They are attempting to get the most value for their money in a manner characteristic of small businesses. However, they wind up failing to accomplish any of their goals because they strive to do too much.

One advertisement, one goal is my general guideline. You should remove everything from the advertisement if it isn't contributing to your goal or aiding in achieving it. This also applies to holy cows, like your brand and emblem. Because advertising space is important, these items are occupying the

Creating a Specialty Product Offer

There is no purpose for many small enterprises to operate. You wouldn't be able to identify them if their name and logo were removed from their website or other promotional materials. Any of the other companies in their industry may be them. Their only purpose is to live and support their owner, who is often barely making ends meet or may not even be able to pay his or her expenses.

From the customer's point of view, they are only there to generate sales and provide no compelling incentive to purchase from them. These kinds of enterprises are prevalent in retail. They exclusively make sales to haphazard walk-in customers. No one is searching them out. Nobody would miss them if they disappeared, and nobody wants what they have to give. Brutal yet accurate.

These companies are merely another "me too" company, which is the issue. How did they determine the cost? How did they choose the merchandise? How were marketing decisions made? Typically, the response is that they just looked at what their closest rival was doing and either duplicated it or made a little adjustment. Please understand that there is nothing wrong with modeling an existing system. That is, in fact, a pretty wise move. But the rival businesses they are emulating may be in the same situation as them—struggling to get business and without a strong argument for you to choose them. Their most consequential commercial moves were based on educated predictions and what their middling rivals were doing. The blind are guiding the other blind.

Eventually, many of these firms "try marketing" after hurting themselves to death for a while, producing just enough money to get by but not enough to thrive. Thus, they begin using an equally dull "me too" pitch to sell their "me too" company. Naturally, it

fails to function. Even the profits from the extra sales they do generate often fall short of paying for their marketing.

The truth is that there is very little probability that you will execute your marketing just right the first time around —message to market and medium match. It's rare for even the most seasoned marketer to win the jackpot on their first attempt. It requires several iterations. To ultimately get your message to the market and media to match correctly, testing and measurement are required.

However, these individuals lack the resources—time, money, and effort—to do it well. Even worse, they have no chance at all if they make a "me too" kind of offer.

Consider marketing as amplification. Here's an illustration. When you tell one person what you do, they don't seem too interested. When you try telling 10 other individuals what you do, they too don't seem enthused. What makes you believe that anything will change even if you use marketing to spread this message to 10,000 people?

Marketing will be difficult if you haven't initially made up your mind as to why your company exists and why customers should choose you over your closest rival.

You must create your USP or unique selling proposition. This is where many people run into difficulties. They make a statement like, "I sell coffee." That is not noteworthy.

Really? So why don't we all simply go to 7-Eleven and get our $1 coffee? Why do we wait in line to pay $4 or $5 for our coffee from a hipster who seems to be in dire need of a bath? Consider it. Typically, you spend between 400% and 500% more for the identical item.

Consider water, which is one of the most plentiful resources on the planet. You gladly pay 2,000 times the price for this commodity when you purchase it in bottled form from a convenience shop or vending machine, as opposed to receiving it from your tap at home.

Observe how the item remains the same in both cases, but the surrounding conditions and elements have altered, or how

Has the way they are delivered and packed changed?

Your USP's main objective is to provide a solution to the following query: Why should I purchase from you instead of your closest rival?

An additional useful test is to see whether people would still recognize your firm or if it could be any other business in your sector if I took away the name and logo from your website.

When creating their USP, individuals often make the mistake of saying that "quality" or "great service" is it. That is incorrect in two ways:

1. Excellent quality and service are expected; they are not special; they are just a component of sound company practices.

2. Customers learn about your excellent quality and service only after they have made a purchase. A strong USP is meant to draw in customers even before they've decided to buy.

When potential customers inquire about pricing at the beginning of the discussion, you know you're promoting your company as a commodity.

Being seen as a commodity and, hence, being judged only on price is a horrible situation for a small company owner to be in. This race to the bottom is undoubtedly going to end in tears because it is heartbreaking.

Creating a distinctive selling proposition is the solution. Something that places you differently from your competition, forcing potential customers to compare you and them side by side.

You're toast if customers can compare you and your rivals on an apples-to-apples basis when it comes to pricing. Someone is always eager to sell for less than you.

Nothing under the sun is new.

The issue, "If there's nothing unique about my business, how do I develop a USP?" is often asked since very few, if any, firms or products are unique.

When assisting my clients in creating their USP, I have two questions for them. The way to marketing and financial success in your company is to answer these two questions.

So, the following are the two questions you need to ask and respond to:

Why should they purchase?

2. Why ought they to purchase from me?

Answers to these kinds of queries have to be precise, succinct, and measurable. Not vague platitudes like "we have the highest quality" or "we are the best."

What special benefit are you providing? Currently, the product itself need not be the source of uniqueness. It's reasonable to argue that there aren't many unique items. How it is marketed, packaged, delivered, or even supported might make it distinctive.

It's important to arrange your company so that, even if your rival were operating just across from you, clients would still choose to do business with you.

If you do it very well, people may even form an overnight queue to transact with you rather than your rival, as they do with Apple items.

Gaining Access to Your Prospect's Mind

Our goal is to understand our prospect's perspective. In reality, what do they want? It's often the outcome of the item you are selling rather than the actual product you are selling. Though small in appearance, the difference is significant.

The purchase of a $50 watch, for instance, is much different from that of a $50,000 watch. In the latter instance, they are probably purchasing exclusivity, luxury, and prestige. Though it's unlikely to be their primary motivator, they do want it to tell the time, just like the person who purchases the $50 watch.

Therefore, we must ascertain what outcome the prospect is purchasing to get insight into their thoughts. After you realize this, you must design your unique selling proposition with the outcome that your target audience is hoping to attain in mind.

If you work as a printer, for instance, you are in the commodities industry. As soon as possible, you wish to leave the commodities industry. While I don't advocate leaving the field, you should adjust your brand positioning.

Instead of selling printing, business cards, and brochures, start asking open-ended queries such as, "Why are you going to a printer? What goals do you have in mind? Prospects are not interested in business cards or pamphlets. They seek the results they believe brochures and business cards will bring to their company.

So, you might sit down with them and say, "What are you trying to accomplish? Together, we will conduct a printing audit to assess all of your printing-related endeavors. You may charge them to do a printing audit by walking them through the procedure. You may then use that consultation fee to cover printing if they decide to choose you to handle their printing. In this manner, you're

no longer thought of as a printer. They now see you as a reliable counsel who meets their demands.

You lose them if you confuse them.

Recognize that your potential customer has three choices:

1. Purchase from you.

2. Purchase from a rival

3. Take no action.

Although you could believe that your largest issue is with your rivals, the truth is that you're probably up against inertia. As a result, you must first respond to their motivation for making a purchase. Next, you must respond to their inquiry about why they ought to purchase from you.

Our generation, known for its sound bites and MTV, is inundated with hundreds of messages every day. There has never been a greater need to produce a message that is both effective and readily comprehensible.

Could you sum up your product's features and special advantages in one sentence?

You need to grasp one crucial idea: misunderstandings result in lost sales. This is particularly true if your product is complicated. A common misconception among company owners is that a perplexed client would ask for an explanation or get in touch with you. There is nothing more false than this. You lose them when you perplex them.

People are seldom motivated enough to sort through a confusing message since they are continually faced with too many alternatives and information.

How to Sell a Commodity in an Unexpected Way

How can you charge a premium for your goods and services and yet have satisfied clients? Simply put, by being exceptional,.

Many company owners say under their breath something like "easier said than done" in response to this response. Maybe this is the case because being exceptional conjures up ideas of being unachievably creative or unique—something that others with

54

considerably more skill do.

The proprietor of the café responds, "Hey, I just sell coffee. How am I expected to be exceptional? That begs the age-old question: how can one be exceptional in the commodity business?

Let's examine a few instances.

Being exceptional does not always include having a one-of-a-kind item or service to provide. Not at all. Being unique may sometimes be risky, challenging, and costly. But you have to be unique. How is the owner of our café different? Look at this:

How much more did the café have to pay to offer art along with coffee? Very close to zero, I would anticipate. Maybe some more training for the barista and a few extra seconds per cup.

However, how many others will each client invite to demonstrate or, much better, tell? Can the proprietor of this café charge fifty cents more per cup than the café across the street? Indeed. That translates to a profit margin of only 50¢ when multiplied by hundreds of thousands of cups annually.

Is the product distinctive, though? Not by a long stretch! It's just barely different, but it's noticeable nonetheless.

Here's an additional illustration. When you purchase on an e-commerce site, you often get the same dull confirmation email. Saying something like, "Your order has been shipped." Tell us if it doesn't come, please. I appreciate your business.

But instead of sending out a generic, uninteresting confirmation email, take a look at how CD Baby delivers a great experience for the consumer and a viral marketing opportunity for themselves:

Using sterile, non-contaminated hands, your CD has been carefully removed from our CD Baby shelf and put on a satin cushion.

Before sending, your CD was examined and polished by a group of fifty workers to ensure it was in the finest possible shape.

As our packaging professional from Japan placed your CD into the most exquisite gold-lined box available, he lit a candle, and the crowd quieted down.

After a fantastic celebration, we all marched down the street to the post office, where Portland as a whole shouted "Bon Voyage!" to your box as it made its way to you on this particular Friday, June 6th, aboard our special CD Baby plane.

I hope your CD Baby purchasing experience was amazing. Yes, we certainly did. We have your photo as the "Customer of the Year" on our wall. Although we're all worn out, we can't wait for you to return to CDBABY.COM!

Thousands of people have shared this purchase confirmation email, and it has been posted on several blogs and websites. The creator of CD Baby, Derek Sivers, attributes thousands of new consumers to this amazing purchase confirmation message.

Again, there's nothing special about the product, but the way it takes something mundane and common and makes it seem special makes the client happy and helps the firm get a free viral promotion.

Here's another example from the very competitive commodities market for consumer electronics:

Like all the other makers of music players at the time, Apple

Cheapest Cost

Sometimes people question me, "Isn't your lowest price your USP?" Yes, that is possible, but can you promise that your prices will be lower than those of all your rivals—including giants like Costco and Walmart—for everything you sell? Not likely.

Someone will always be willing to close their company sooner than you.

I advise against playing the game.

A USP that claims to have the lowest pricing on certain items isn't nearly as appealing.

It's a truth that small and medium-sized businesses are unlikely to outbid the large discounters on pricing.

To be honest, you most likely don't want to. You may draw in higher-quality customers by raising your rates. Contrary to popular belief, you get considerably fewer complaints from high-end clients than from low-end ones. I've seen and encountered this at a variety of companies in a variety of sectors.

Adding value to your product is a preferable strategy over discounting. Adding services, personalizing the solution, and bundling incentives may all create real value for your consumer at very little additional expense to you.

Additionally, it facilitates the creation of that crucial apples-to-oranges comparison that frees you from the commodities game.

Don't hate the player; despise the game. So, do your hardest not to play the commodity/price game. Create your USP, execute it, and get the people you work with to participate on your terms.

Make your pitch for an elevator.

Being able to communicate the issue you address as a company owner is an art, particularly if your industry is complicated.

Making an "elevator pitch" is an excellent method of condensing your USP. An elevator pitch is a succinct, practiced synopsis of your company and its value proposition that can be given in between thirty and ninety seconds or the length of an elevator trip.

Although it may seem corny and you may not use it often as

an elevator pitch, it can be a very useful tool for emphasizing your message and unique selling point. We'll talk about this in a moment, but as you start creating your offer, this will become quite useful.

The thirty seconds that follow after someone asks, "What do you do?" are among the most often squandered marketing chances. The answer is almost always evasive, contradictory, and self-serving.

Many respond with the most impressive-sounding title they can manage at this point because they believe the questioner's assessment of their value will be based on their response. "My title is waste management technician," the cleaner declares.

One lady told me she was a senior event builder when I inquired what she did for a livelihood. Not knowing what she did, I kept asking questions until I eventually realized that she set up seats for stadium events like concerts.

While it's true that some superficial individuals base their opinion of someone's value on their occupation or industry, there's a far better method to answer this question, and it doesn't need you to use a thesaurus to distort or obscure what you do.

When someone inquires about your line of work, that's your chance to give a brief elevator speech. It's the ideal chance to regularly spread your marketing message in a variety of contexts.

You want to avoid coming off as a pushy, annoying salesman; therefore, it's critical to organize your elevator pitch well. The majority of elevator pitches have the same issue as exaggerated job titles. Instead of impressing the receiver, it leaves them perplexed or thinking, "What a douchebag."

Ineffective marketing is mostly self- and product-focused. Our elevator pitch should be customer-, problem-, and solution-focused since this is the hallmark of effective marketing, particularly direct response marketing. Rather than for some great but cryptic title or industry, we want to be recognized for the problems we tackle.

Effective marketing leads the potential customer on a path that addresses the issue, the fix, and the evidence at the end. Likewise, your elevator pitch needs to be.

In around thirty seconds, how can these three elements be communicated effectively? I've found that the best formula is: You know [the problem]? We, however, provide a solution. As a matter of fact, [proof].

Here are a few instances:

Insurance Sales: "You know how most people rarely review their insurance coverage when their circumstances change? My job is to ensure that people's insurance coverage is appropriate for their present situation, which helps them feel more at ease. My customer was robbed only last week, but since his insurance was current, he was able to get back the whole worth of the goods he had lost.

Electrical Engineering: "Are you aware of the instances in which major corporations' vital systems are brought down by power outages? I, therefore, construct backup power systems for businesses whose activities depend on a steady supply of electricity. I set up the system at XYZ Bank.

This means that since the system was implemented, they have had 100% uptime.

Website Development: "You know how most company websites are out of date? What I do is install software that enables users to easily update their websites without having to hire a web designer regularly. In reality, I just implemented the program for a customer, and they were able to avoid paying $2,000 a year for web development.

This provides you with an effective technique for creating an elevator pitch that is problem- or customer-focused rather than you- or product-focused.

Formulating Your Offer

Here is the most important aspect, and here is when many individuals get lazy and provide something uninteresting, undercut their competitors' prices, or just mimic what their closest rival is doing.

Recall that your ideal target market will prioritize pricing above all other considerations when making decisions if you don't provide them with a convincing argument for why your offer is unique. After all, given the available facts, which apple would you choose if vendor A was selling them for $1 while vendor B was offering what seemed to be identical apples for $1.50?

It is your responsibility to develop a compelling offer that stands out from those of your rivals.

When you're creating your offer, these are two excellent questions to consider:

1. Which of the goods and services you provide do you feel most confident in your ability to deliver? For instance, what kind of good or service would you provide if you were only compensated once the customer received the intended outcome? Put another way, what issue do you feel certain you could resolve for a customer in your target market?

2. Which of the goods and services you provide do you most like delivering?

You may improve your offer by asking yourself more questions, like: What exactly is my target market buying? For instance, consumers purchase peace of mind rather than insurance. Which is the greatest advantage to start with? Which emotionally charged words and phrases work best to draw in and keep this market's attention? What concerns do my potential customers have, and how will I address them? What ridiculous offer am I allowed to make, together with a guarantee? Is there a captivating tale I could share? Who else, and how, is making equivalent sales of my goods or services? Who else has attempted to sell something comparable to this target market, and why did that attempt fail?

A primary cause of marketing campaign failure is a haphazard and poorly considered proposition. It's something like 10% or 20% off, which is awful and boring.

One of the most crucial components of any marketing campaign is the offer; therefore, you should invest a lot of time and effort into making sure it is structured properly.

What Desires My Target Audience?

One of the first marketing errors that entrepreneurs make is putting the incorrect material in front of the appropriate audience or the right material in front of the wrong audience.

For this reason, determining a precise target market for our marketing initiatives is the focus of the first and maybe most crucial square of the one-page marketing plan.

After laying the foundation, we want to design an offer that will pique the interest of our target market. One that will have them eager to take out their money and one that will stand out from all the monotonous, lazy offerings from our rivals.

Asking your prospects is one of the simplest ways to find out what they want. Either a survey or more formal market research will achieve this.

Furthermore, it should be mentioned that most individuals are unaware of their desires until they are given them. Additionally, individuals use reason when filling out questionnaires or responding to market research, but they also use emotion when making purchases, which they then justify with reason. Thus, you must add observation to your questioning.

Those looking to purchase pricey luxury vehicles would usually respond with rationale (but false or partially accurate) statements about what they needed in terms of comfort, quality, and dependability. Prestige is what they want.

Henry Ford is quoted as saying, "If I had asked people what they wanted, they would have said faster horses." This is a great way to put it.

An effective method for doing market research is to examine what your target market is purchasing or searching for.

Examine the goods and niches that are popular on websites such as eBay and Amazon.

Another great technique is to analyze search engine queries using a program like Google's AdWords Keyword Planner.

Finally, check out the subjects that are popular on business news websites and social media. What are people responding to and making comments about?

By using these tools, you may get an understanding of what is presently in demand and being discussed or pondered like tapping into the global consciousness.

Make a compelling offer

You need to bundle what your market wants and present it as an alluring offer now that you know what they want. Here are a few of the crucial components:

Value: To start, consider what would be the most beneficial item you could provide your client. What is the outcome that allows you to guide them from point A to point B while still turning a healthy profit?

This is the essence of what you are offering.

Language: You must get familiar with the terminology and language used in your target market if you are not a part of it. Talk about "endos," "sick wheelies," and "bunny hops" instead of features, advantages, and specs if you're marketing BMX bikes. When marketing golf clubs, you must discuss "hooks," "slices," and "handicaps."

Reason for doing this: You must explain your actions while making a fantastic offer. People are so used to being taken advantage of that they become suspicious and search for the catch when someone presents a compelling offer that seems full of value.

In one of my firms, we were providing a much superior service at a cost that was almost half that of our rivals. I have firsthand experience with this. Calls to the sales line were coming in, asking what the catch was and summarizing the offer that was posted online.

Although I wouldn't advise you to make up an excuse for your offer, be prepared with a good one. Some examples include getting rid of outdated or broken merchandise, overstocking, relocating your office or warehouse, and so on.

Value stacking: provide a ton of incentives to make your offer seem compelling. This is a really wise strategy that may significantly boost conversions. I think that the bonuses should be worth more than the

primary offer, if at all feasible. Infomercials excel at doing this. "That's not all...", "We'll double your offer," and so on.

Upsells: This is the ideal moment to provide a related product or service to a hot prospect who is in the market. Even if the main product you are selling has a low margin, this is the ideal time to add a high-profit item. It's the burger and fries, the longer warranty, and the rustproofing of the automobile. You make more money with each transaction, and the client receives value additions.

Payment plan: this one is particularly crucial for high-ticket products and may be the difference between the buyer balking and walking away or completing the transaction.

Presenting a $5,000 item in 12 convenient installments of $497 helps the buyer swallow the expense much more easily. People typically budget their costs monthly, so $497 a month seems much more manageable than $5,000 all at once.

Moreover, note that the total of 12 x $497 is greater than $5,000. It approaches $6,000. If you're financing the transaction, your primary motivation for doing this is to pay your borrowing expenses.

Secondly, you want to reward those who can pay all at once by offering them a "discount" for making their payment in full.

promise: as this chapter's earlier discussion indicated, you need a ridiculous promise. One that completely flips the risk associated with doing business with you. People don't accept any of your statements since they have been let down so many times. Nothing about it is personal. That's the nature of things. Dealing with you should be risk-free; if you don't follow through on your commitments, the onus should be on you. "Satisfaction guaranteed" is a flimsy and useless promise.

Scarcity: There must be a sense of scarcity in your offer, something that compels consumers to act right away. Fear of losing affects people much more than the possibility of gain. But once again, you must have a solid "reason."

You don't want to be dishonest in your scarcity assertions; therefore, you should explain "why" the shortage exists.

You are working with limited resources, time, and supplies. Make the most of this for your marketing. Having a constant countdown of the remaining time or supply available might intensify the feeling of fear of loss.

As you've seen, creating an intriguing offer requires a lot of work. Choosing the careless, inconsiderate route of "10% off" or other such cheap deals is like tossing your marketing money in the garbage.

Spend some time developing a strong, well-considered offer. Your conversion rate will rise, and so will your profit line.

Focus on the pain.

You've got a splitting headache. You open your medicine cabinet and start sifting through your museum of half-used pills, lotions, and vitamins, only to find you're entirely out of pain relief medicines. Thus, you go to your neighborhood drugstore in the hopes of finding the medication that would provide you with much-needed relief.

Are you concerned about the cost? Does it ever occur to you to check at other pharmacies to see if you can get the same product for less money? Not likely. You need quick relief since you're in agony. Would you purchase the pills even if they were twice or three times as expensive as usual?

When we're in pain, our normal buying habits are abandoned. This also applies to your prospects and consumers. Businesses tend to focus more on features and perks than on addressing the problems that customers are already facing. How much persuasion does a pharmacist have to give someone suffering from a splitting headache before they purchase painkillers? Very little, I believe.

Whether you sell TVs, vehicles, or consulting, the same applies. There are consumers and possibilities for you that are suffering. Not features and perks, but pain alleviation is what they desire.

If you were trying to sell me a TV, you may attempt to convince me of its features and advantages by mentioning things like its four HDMI connections and 4K resolution. For most individuals, this will mean very little. Instead, picture yourself focusing on my biggest complaint, which is having to get it home, unpack it, and then spend many hours trying to get it to sync with all of my other gadgets.

Why not offer to send it to my home, mount it on the wall, make sure the image quality is amazing, and make sure it functions flawlessly with all of my peripherals instead of cutting prices and treating yourself like a commodity? You're relieving my discomfort now, and the cost goes down.

more significant than if you were trying to sell me a product with a long list of features and advantages.

In the aforementioned example, you may be offering the same TV as your rival, but if you package it in a manner that alleviates my suffering, you have my business. Additionally, since you weren't simply a commodity seller, there's a much higher chance that I'll become a raving fan and recommend you to others. You were a problem-solver. This is now a comparison of apples and oranges. In what way does this differ from "having four HDMI ports and 4K resolution"?

The best approach to converting potential customers into price shoppers who see your product as a commodity purchased only based on price is to sell features and advantages. Being a pain reliever and issue solution is your aim, as is making any comparison with your rivals seem like apples to oranges. Recall that individuals are much more prepared to spend money on a cure than on prevention. Reducing price resistance, increasing consumer happiness, and increasing conversion are all achieved by addressing current suffering rather than promising future pleasure. Seek out areas of concern for your sector and provide solutions.

Copywriting for Sales: You Can't Make People Buy Anything by Bore Them

Writing powerful words will pay you much more than almost any other talent. The ultimate marketing talent is knowing exactly why a potential customer should choose you above your rivals and how to say it in a manner that makes them feel something and spurs them on to action.

We said before in this book that copywriting for direct response marketing is significantly different. We employ content in direct response marketing that is intended to hit the target audience's emotional hot buttons.

Instead of using text that is traditional, dull, and "professional" sounding, we utilize copy that makes you want to look at it even when you don't want to.

Strong sales copy, attention-grabbing headlines, and persuasive calls to action are all part of emotional direct response copywriting. It's referred to as "print salesmanship."

Many companies believe that this kind of content is inappropriate for their market, particularly those that cater to professional or corporate clients. Furthermore, it would be a grave error to undervalue emotional direct response copywriting, even though it is true that we should customize our strategy for this market as we would for any target market.

We're all major emotional consumers, regardless of our position —from the CEO of a Fortune 500 firm to the janitor—and we base our purchasing choices on feelings that are subsequently supported by reason. "Hey honey, safety is the main reason I bought that Porsche 911, and German automobiles are also very dependable." Yes, exactly.

When I meet company owners face-to-face, I often discover that their personalities are very different from those portrayed in their marketing. Most of them don't even show any personality in their marketing.

because they believe they must project a "professional" image. Their advertising is often dull and generic; if you were to replace their name and emblem on any of their promotional materials, it could be any other company in the same sector. It's a pity since they might achieve far more success if their marketing spoke to consumers the same way they do in person.

These individuals are often quite clever, fascinating to talk to, and enthusiastic about what they do when you meet them in person, but it seems like they go blank when it comes to their sales copy and marketing materials. They start utilizing weasel words and phrases they would never typically employ in conversation in an attempt to seem "professional" all of a sudden. Words and phrases like "best-of-breed products," "synergistic," "strategic alignment," and similar expressions are what I mean. Words they would never say with friends or coworkers in a genuine discussion

Individuals purchase from other individuals, not from companies; that is a reality. In the realm of one-to-one sales, building rapport and connections is widely recognized. But, for some reason, many company owners believe they must suppress their personalities and act like a faceless corporation while working in the one-to-many role of marketing. Copywriting is print salesmanship. Your sales copy should be written as if you were speaking with a single individual.

Creating dull, monotonous, and "professional" sales copy is the quickest way to turn off prospects and consumers. Claims of being the top supplier in your industry and meaningless platitudes make you seem like a "me too" company. "Me too" companies get the lowest-common-denominator customers who, because they have nothing else to set you apart from them, must buy on price.

People like opinions, personalities, and honesty. Even if they disagree with you, they will still value your candor and authenticity. In a sea of sameness and monotony, being unique and showcasing your individuality can help you stand out. Take a peek at one of the longest-running TV shows ever.

formats—the news anchor who speaks. Why would you spend so much airtime displaying the presenter's face? A lot more information and visual footage of news stories could be aired if they just provided voiceovers.

Still, the talking head takes up a lot of time since it presents issues that are typically boring to some personalities. It also exudes authority and has the sense of a private discussion with a reliable source. Images and videos of other people elicit reactions from humans. The fact that Facebook and YouTube are two of the most popular websites in the world is no coincidence. We pay great attention to the words and deeds of others.

This is something that you can readily use for your company. Including a video on your website is one example. Using a portable camera or even a smartphone, you can quickly record and publish a five-minute video that consists of you introducing your goods and services. Using social media as a two-way channel of communication to interact with clients and prospects is another example. By incorporating these two simple actions into your company, you'll be fostering stronger relationships.

Don't hide behind your marketing materials as a screen. Use it to share your thoughts, observations, counsel, and comments, but most of all, just be genuine to yourself. By doing this, you will establish rapport right away and set yourself apart from the other dull, uninteresting marketing collateral that is out there.

When reading an email, people open their mail atop a wastepaper bin and place their index finger just above the delete button. They separate their mail into two piles: the first is read and opened, and the second, which is often left unread, is thrown in the garbage. People are in the mood for something novel, interesting, and novel. You attract their attention when you offer them that. When your writing is "professional," it is monotonous, uninteresting, and unread. The truth is that most companies are too frightened to send out correspondence that

will draw attention to them. They are afraid of what their friends, family, colleagues in business, and others may say or think.

Thus, they publish shy and relatable messages and advertisements. If you were to alter the firm name and logo, it would essentially be identical to all of its rivals. Your customers' and prospects' opinions are the only ones you should be concerned about. Quite frankly, your sales copy shouldn't take into account the opinions of anybody else, not even yourself. The only accurate approach to assessing the impact of your content is to test it and gauge reaction.

The majority of people lead quiet, desperate lives. Even if it's just for a little while, they are utterly in need of anything that captures their attention or amuses them. You must provide it to them.

Take Over the Discussion Your Prospect Is Currently Having

Everybody is always having a mental dialogue with themselves. This is known as "inner talk" at times.

A pregnant mother and a retiree will have quite different conversations in that regard. Or for a couch slug who is also an obsessive exercise devotee. For this reason, it's critical to have a thorough understanding of your target market.

One target audience type will not be interested in an emotional hot button that another would find offensive. Writing content that elicits strong emotions from readers is not a replacement for knowing exactly who your target audience is and what their emotional triggers are.

You must have a thorough understanding of your target market's thought processes, linguistic preferences, daily routines, and internal dialogue before you write a single word of content. What worries and annoys them? What motivates and excites them?

Research is sometimes the most overlooked aspect of copywriting and is the main cause of occasionally unsuccessful results, even with effective text. One of the most effective tools in your marketing toolbox is emotional direct response copywriting. But realize that it's a step in the process. If you do your research, write, test, and measure, you'll be miles ahead of 99.9% of your rivals.

Addressing the elephant in the room is another way to get your prospect to start talking about you. It's only natural to sell yourself by continually attempting to show your company in the best possible light. But this often results in one of the most typical marketing errors: talking only about the advantages of doing business with you. It's a rookie error to ignore the hazards involved in purchasing from you or the "elephant in the room."

The fear center of our brain is called the amygdala. It controls how we respond to situations that are crucial to our survival and incites dread to alert us to impending danger. Your amygdala is active at night when you are being followed by someone who seems suspicious, and your heart is racing. That's excellent. But your prospect's amygdala may also dissuade them from purchasing from you. That is not good.

Whether you run a hospital or a coffee shop, when a potential client is thinking about purchasing from you, their amygdala is weighing the dangers. The danger that the amygdala is assessing might be as little as a bad-tasting coffee or as serious as an early death when a patient is on the operating table. In any case, the risk assessment is continuously ongoing in the background. You have to realize it as a marketer and owner of a firm. By avoiding this topic in your marketing, you may ruin the sale by letting your prospect's amygdala go crazy. Since you can't avoid this risk assessment, why not take part and offer yourself the greatest opportunity to handle any possible deal breakers before they have a chance to negatively impact your financial line?

Conventional sales practices advise us to overcome objections, yet in practice, objections are seldom raised. Instead, we say stupid things like "Let me think about it" in our polite society, but deep down, the amygdala is screaming, "Let's get out of here." Informing prospective customers of the people your product or service is not for is part of writing effective sales copy. There are three excellent reasons for taking this action.

It does this by first eliminating individuals who are outside of your target market or who are not a suitable match for what you have to offer. This guarantees you don't waste time on prospects that are low-quality and low-probability. Additionally, it lessens the quantity of returns and concerns from clients who didn't understand what they had purchased.

Second, telling them who this thing is intended for instantly lends it more credibility. When you cover both, it seems much more impartial.

angles by stating to them who it is and isn't intended for.

Finally, if you say your product or service is for everyone, prospects will feel it is more specifically customized to meet their requirements than if you say it is for everyone. It seems more exclusive and focused.

Finding out what your prospect is blaming and using the "enemy in common" approach in your content are two more great ways to get inside their heads. When most individuals are asked why they haven't succeeded, some of the most typical answers are as follows: The financial system The administration There are too many taxes. inadequate parenting or upbringing unhelpful friends or relatives Not enough money, time, or opportunity Absence of knowledge or training Unjust manager

They aren't on this list, which is the only issue with it!

Here are the findings of a nationwide poll on "cost-of-living pressure," often referred to as spending too much and earning too little, that was carried out by one of the main newspapers. Very few individuals hold themselves responsible for their present situation.

The Journal of Safety Research reports that 74% of Americans think they drive better than average. However, only 1% think they are not good enough.

It's the same with taking responsibility. How often have you heard a young person say, "It's not my fault"? People are very much the same as adults. The majority of us don't think we're at fault. What, then, can you do with this information? First, never hold your prospects responsible for the

the situation they're in. No matter how different these current thinking processes are from our own, our marketing message must consider them if we want to join the dialogue now taking place in their brains.

"The enemy in common" is an excellent strategy for capitalizing on the "It's not my fault" mindset. Choose a pertinent issue from your prospect's list of grievances, take their side, and use it to support the solution you have to offer. An example headline for an accountant maybe this one:

"Complimentary Guide Explains How to Take Back Your Hard-Earned Money from the Jealous Tax Collector"

Providing a solution to your prospect while building a relationship with them is a terrific strategy. By connecting with the prospect via a shared adversary, you may position yourself as the one standing up to an opponent, in this instance, government taxation.

"The enemy in common" shakes their cage, interrupts the mental dialogue, and arouses the feelings that are simmering under the surface.

It's a fantastic method to stand out from the crowd and capture your prospect's interest.

How to Name Your Business, Service, or Product

I've had several "naming discussion" sessions with business owners. Typically, I'm asked to weigh in on a new name or various names that may be proposed for a new product, service, or enterprise. An explanation of the name or names under consideration usually comes next. Here's my opinion on naming: in my opinion, it is always a failure if you have to explain the name. There should be equal substance in the title. Put another way, you're beginning from behind if the name doesn't immediately convey what the good, service, or company is. Some shake their heads in shock when I offer them this counsel. What about well-known companies with odd names like Apple, Amazon, Skype, Nike, and so forth? Surely, by offering such basic guidance, I must be missing something? This is the issue. The major businesses all invest hundreds of millions of dollars in advertising to tell the public about their identities and products. To what extent would you be willing to pay to follow suit?

We're not even discussing advertising that closes deals or produces leads here. We are discussing advertising that just summarizes your services. There is no greater financial waste, in my opinion. You're beginning at a disadvantage when you choose a non-obvious name, and you'll have to pay a lot of money for advertising to catch up. All you needed to do to save yourself this enormous financial waste was to rename your company "Fast Plumbing Repairs," which clarifies your mission and values right away, as opposed to "Aqua Solutions," which requires you to explain that the name "Aqua Solutions" comes from the Latin word "aqua," which means "water," and that you offer "complete plumbing solutions" (whatever that means).

I've encountered company names and product names with ambiguous meanings much too often. There are instances when it's cheesy wordplay, instances when it's a hidden literary allusion, and instances when it's a made-up term with an unclear meaning.

of which is only obvious to the developer. The truth is, very few people will take the time to attempt to figure out the origin or meaning of your name, no matter how brilliant it is. These may be significant to you since your company is your pride and joy, but very seldom do clients or potential clients even consider them.

Even worse, trying to be "clever" usually backfires and causes misunderstandings. As we discussed before in this chapter, sales are lost due to misunderstandings. If you confuse them, you lose them. It's that simple. Always prefer clarity over ingenuity. Even under the best of circumstances, getting a message received, comprehended, and then acted upon may be difficult. However, it's insane to purposefully introduce uncertainty into the mix when your tiny firm has a limited marketing budget.

Finally, don't ask your loved ones what they think of your smart new name. Of course, you'll get compliments and applause for your concept, which makes you feel good, but it's unlikely to be beneficial. By all means, test the waters and get feedback, but do it from unbiased individuals inside your target market, not from those who are already familiar with your offerings. Give it some time and effort, and most of all, concentrate on clarity. Naming may work for you or against you, and it's costly and hard to modify later on.

CHAPTER 3: USING ADVERTISING MEDIA TO REACH PROSPECTS

USING ADVERTISING MEDIA
TO REACH PROSPECTS

One of the greatest marketers, John Wanamaker, is credited as saying, "Half the money I spend on advertising is wasted; the trouble is I don't know which half..."

When this was originally stated a century ago, it made sense, but saying it now ought to be illegal. However, the majority of small firms monitor their advertising very little, if at all. It is indicative of an amateur to not monitor ROI on ad expenditure and to not measure the source of leads and revenues. With the use of technology, we can all simply, swiftly, and affordably monitor the success of our advertisements.

This is straightforward thanks to tools like discount codes, internet analytics, and toll-free lines. Keep in mind that management follows measurement. Spend your advertising money ruthlessly, riding the winners and slashing the losers. Monitoring and measuring are necessary to determine what is winning and what is losing.

Because media is by far the most costly part of your marketing budget, this is essential. It serves as the link between your target market and your offer. You must be aware of the peculiarities of each kind of media, whether you're utilizing more modern digital platforms like social media, email marketing, and search engine optimization (SEO) or more conventional ones like radio, TV, and print.

To go into the technical specifics of each media type and subcategory would be much beyond the purview of this work. But I would advise you to do the following generally: Employ specialists in whatever medium you determine is appropriate for your campaign; they are invaluable. Particularly when it comes to the most costly step in your marketing strategy, don't attempt to do it yourself. It will harm you to not know. Whether you use offline media like direct mail, print, or radio, or online media like social media, email, or the web, each has its quirks and technicalities that you are very likely to screw up if you are not familiar with them. If you have the ideal target market and offer in place, it would be tragic if your campaign failed due to a technical error in your media.

I am asked this kind of thing all the time: "What's a good response rate for direct mail?" or "When using email marketing, what kind of open rate should I anticipate?" It's expected of me to respond with a number. Say something along the lines of, "Expect a 20% open rate for email and a 2% response rate from direct mail."

These inquiries are often made by well-intentioned company owners who are still developing their marketing strategy. It depends on how I always respond to it. A 50% response rate may sometimes spell catastrophe, while a 0.01% response rate can occasionally spell enormous success.

Response rates may differ significantly based on several variables, including the message's relevance to the target market, the offer's persuasiveness, and the method used to get the list you are marketing to. Rather than posing the absurd question of "What is a good response rate?" they should be asking, "How do I measure the success of my marketing campaign?"

So, how can the effectiveness of a marketing strategy be determined?

For those who lack patience, the quick response is as follows: did the marketing effort bring in more revenue than it took? Put another way, what was the marketing campaign's return on investment (ROI)? It's a failure if the expenses exceed the profits you have earned or will ever make from this campaign.

It's a success if the expenses you incurred are less than the campaign's earnings.

Naturally, many would disagree with me and claim that even a financially unsuccessful campaign was worthwhile because it "got your name out there" or served as a kind of "branding" exercise. The likelihood is that you cannot afford to spend tens of millions of dollars on nebulous marketing such as "branding" or "getting your name out there" unless you are a major brand like Nike, Apple, Coca-Cola, or something like that.

You'll do significantly better by focusing on putting your prospects' names in here rather than "getting your name out there."

Marketing budgets are what I like to think of as firepower. To hunt effectively, return home triumphantly, and provide for your family, you must make prudent use of your limited amount of weaponry. But you'll surprise and frighten your target if you start shooting aimlessly in all directions. If you want to succeed, you must be astute and focused.

For small and medium-sized businesses, it is essential to get a return on investment from their marketing expenses. Investing your very little marketing budget in fuzzy marketing would be like a child urinating in the sea.

Atomic bomb-scale firepower is the only way to win the game of mass marketing, branding, and publicizing your identity. That's not a game you can play if you own a small or medium-sized company. Given this, we must carefully examine the statistics.

Let's go over an example using some numerical data to better understand. For the sake of clarity, I'll keep the figures modest and rounded. You send out 100 letters as part of a direct mail campaign. $300 will be spent on printing and sending the 100 letters. Ten people reply to each of the 100 letters sent (10% response rate).

Two of the ten respondents end up purchasing from you (20% closing rate).

We can calculate the client acquisition cost—one of the most significant figures in marketing—from this. In this case, the campaign brought you two new clients for a total cost of $300. Thus, $150 is your client acquisition cost.

This was a losing campaign, however, if the product or service you provide to these clients only brings in $100 for each transaction. For each new consumer you brought in with this marketing, you lost $50 (negative ROI).

But this is a successful campaign, provided the product or service you offer generates a profit of $600 for each transaction. For each new client you brought on, you earned $450 (positive ROI).

This is a very basic example, but it shows how meaningless conversion and response rates and other data are. The return on investment, which fluctuates depending on the cost of acquiring new customers and the real profit a marketing campaign generates, is our main concern.

Focusing on a specialty has several benefits, not the least of which is that marketing becomes considerably more affordable. Because there is a lot less waste, targeted advertising ends up being far less expensive than bulk marketing.

Advertising in New Mother Magazine is a considerably better option if you're selling newborn baby photographs than placing a generic photography ad in the classifieds.

Because your message-to-market fit is considerably better and your conversion rate is greater than if your ad had a generic message, your cost per client acquisition will decrease significantly.

Your narrower target market would also result in cheaper

advertising expenditures for you.

Recall that the whole point of your advertisement is to get your potential customer to say, "Hey, that's for me."

It is improbable that attempting to please everyone would get the same response.

The customer's "front end," "back end," and lifetime value

Using the provided example, we were able to conclude that our campaign was unsuccessful if we were only making $100 profit per transaction. But in that case, we neglected to include client lifetime value, another crucial metric for evaluating the effectiveness of marketing campaigns.

The campaign's economics are entirely altered if, for instance, we get $100 straight from the campaign and the buyer keeps making purchases from us thereafter. Considering the lifetime worth of a client might turn a campaign that seemed to be a loss into a success.

We now have to consider the potential profit margin for a client throughout their relationship with us. You may sell cars that need to be serviced, printers that need to be refilled, or anything else that people often purchase, including haircuts, massages, Internet access, insurance, and so on.

"The front end" refers to the upfront revenue we get from a campaign. "The back end" is the money we earn from further purchases. The sum of these numbers represents a customer's lifetime worth.

Two essential figures you must understand to assess the efficacy of your marketing are lifetime value and client acquisition cost. The response and conversion rates, among other data, are meaningless by themselves. We only use them to calculate these two metrics, which provide us with an accurate view of the effectiveness of our marketing.

It's time to start tracking and holding your marketing responsible if you don't already know what these figures are in your company. A high-growth firm is built on continuous testing, measurement, and improvement of these metrics.

The offer that prospects—those who aren't yet your customers—see is your "front-end" offer. They have no reason to like or trust you since they don't know you. Creating a client and making enough money from the first transaction to at least offset the expense of acquiring the consumer are the main objectives of your front-end offer. This makes continuing to advertise quite viable. The "back end" is where the true profit is created when returning consumers make more purchases.

In some cases, it makes sense to "go negative" or lose money upfront since you can be sure you'll make up for it and then some. This is often the case for companies that provide subscription services or have high lifetime values. Stick to the objective of having your front end pay for your client acquisition costs until you have a firm grasp on your lifetime value figures. If you don't know your statistics, this might be a hazardous approach. We will go further into the back end and boost client lifetime value in Chapter 8. This has the power to transform your company and make unsuccessful efforts successful.

Is Social Media the Magic Bullet?

The Internet and social media are unquestionably media innovations. They have enabled an unparalleled degree of connectivity and democratized information. On the other hand, these so-called "new media" also come with a healthy dose of hype. Given the amount of hoopla around social media, one would think it was a panacea for marketing. Many self-described "gurus" of social media would have you think that social media is the way of the future for all marketing and that you're a Luddite who will go out of business soon if you don't devote most or all of your marketing efforts to social media.

Naturally, like with most hype, it's important to maintain objectivity while trying to distinguish reality from fantasy. Let me clear the air before I'm called out for being anti-social media. I've worked with social media at several different firms and still use it often.

But since social media is getting so much attention, I want to help you understand how it fits into a larger marketing plan and put it into context.

To be effective, a marketing effort must meet three essential criteria:

1. Market: the intended audience for your message (discussed in Chapter 1) 2. Message: the offer or marketing message you deliver (discussed in Chapter 2)

3. Media (explained in this chapter): the channel by which you communicate with your target audience; examples include TV, radio, direct mail, telemarketing, the Internet, and so on.

To have a good campaign, you must hit all three of these. You must use the appropriate medium to communicate with the appropriate target audience.

channel. If you fall short on any of these three fronts, your marketing strategy is likely to fail. Contextualizing information is made easier by knowing this framework. Social media is not a plan; it is, by definition, a kind of media.

The emergence of a new media outlet does not instantly alter the tried-and-true principles of marketing. Is this the appropriate medium for your business? is the next question to consider. Recall that one of the three aspects we must master for a campaign to succeed is the media. Social media is much like any other medium in that it has its quirks. Here are a few social media-related cautions you should be aware of:

It's hardly the best setting for selling, to start. Social networking is best compared to a party or get-together, in my opinion. Everybody has attended events where someone—possibly a friend or family member—has fallen victim to the multi-level marketing enigma. You know, the part where they attempt to sell or enlist others to sell by touting the health advantages of the newest pills or potions?

Everyone finds it awkward, as it seems forced and like the wrong moment to be giving or receiving a sales pitch. It is precisely the same with social media. In general, overt marketing and persistent offer pitching are seen as bad conduct on social media and may work against your brand by turning customers away rather than drawing them in.

However, social media is a terrific way to establish and grow connections that, if a good match, may eventually evolve into something commercial, just like in a real-life social gathering. Getting a sense of how consumers feel about your company and interacting with outspoken customers who voice their opinions in a public arena are two of the most useful things I see on social media.

Social evidence is a bonus that comes with this. Building social proof by being approachable, answering compliments and criticism, and interacting with your clientele gives prospects and customers the impression that they are working with real people rather than a faceless company. Remember, people purchase from people.

With social media, there are two possible pitfalls.

It might be a time-waster to start. It may be exhausting to feel as if you have to reply to every stupid remark. It can also take time away from marketing duties, which can provide a far higher return on investment in terms of both time and money. It's critical to use social media with self-control. You can't allow yourself or them to get carried away with the online counterpart, just as you wouldn't let your staff members hang around and gossip all day. Social media marketing is seen as "free" by some individuals. It's only really free if you don't value your time at all.

There is also the ownership issue. In reality, the social network owns your profile and page on their platform. Therefore, investing a significant amount of time and resources into developing a profile and following these networks ultimately enhances their strengths rather than your own.

Building and owning my marketing assets, such as websites, blogs, email lists, and the like, is what I would love to do whenever feasible. Then, I just utilize social media to increase traffic to these promotional materials. In this manner, I can devote my time and energy to remodeling my own "home" instead of a landlord who has the power to evict me at any moment.

Facebook's policy change regarding business pages serves as an excellent illustration of why you should take this action. Previously, you could access this whole audience for free if they "liked" your company's Facebook page. Thus, companies invested a great deal of time, resources, and energy into encouraging individuals to "like" their Facebook page.

Facebook now demands payment from you every time you want to communicate with your whole audience. If not, it just lets you get a small portion of the audience. This was a devastating blow to individuals who had invested a great deal of money in growing their Facebook following just to have it ripped out from under them.

For this reason, out of 10,000 individuals who "like" my Facebook page, I would rather have 1,000 people on my email list.

As with any marketing plan, it's critical to identify the places where your prospects "hang out" and to utilize the right medium to reach them with your message. They could hang out in locations other than social media.

Email Promotion

A direct and intimate method of communicating with clients and prospects is via email. Almost everyone carries or has ready access to email due to the widespread use of smartphones and other mobile devices.

Creating an email subscriber database is essential to any internet marketing plan. A conspicuous email opt-in form on your website is a must. This lets you get website visitors' email addresses and allows you to follow up with interested parties who may not be ready to purchase right away but would still want further information.

Lead nurturing and lead acquisition are two essential phases in the marketing process, as we'll cover in the following two chapters. They enable us to engage with potential customers in an informed manner, even if they aren't ready to make a purchase just yet. Generally, these sorts of prospects make up the bulk of all prospects and are critical to filling your pipeline of future sales. You would probably lose these interested but unpurchased customers forever if you didn't attract them. All you could hope for is that when they did decide to purchase, out of all the hundreds of websites they may have visited, they would remember yours and finish the purchasing cycle they started days, weeks, or months before.

Moreover, email allows you to be in constant communication with your clientele and facilitates the testing and introduction of new goods and services. As you establish a rapport with your email list members, your database grows in value as a marketing tool.

You may make money on demand by building an email

subscriber list that is very responsive. You draft an enticing offer, including a way for people to respond, and send a broadcast email to your list. You get prompt feedback about the success or failure of the offer. It's an excellent method of

affordable testing proposals before investing in more costly media, such as print or pay-per-click advertising.

Any database of email subscribers is still one of the most crucial components of any Internet marketing plan, even with the rise in popularity of social media. Because so few of your followers will see your message, social media reach has become problematic, as we've seen in the preceding few pages. You would most likely be lost in the din of noise even if your message were to reach everyone. Jokes, memes, and funny cat videos will overpower your marketing pitch. It's called social media for a reason.

What's more, an email database is a property that you own. It is not reliant on whatever trendy social networking platform happens to be at the moment. Do you remember MySpace? Even though I don't believe Facebook or Twitter will disappear anytime soon, the industry is changing quickly. Should you establish your company on someone else's platform and it begins to lose appeal, your most valuable internet marketing resource will be left behind.

Email has a few quirks that you should be aware of, despite its effectiveness as a medium. Here are a few important email-related dos and don'ts:

Avoid spamming. In most countries, email marketing is governed by stringent regulations. Most importantly, to send marketing emails to an email recipient, you need their permission. An opt-in form on your website is thus essential. If the receivers haven't specifically asked to be addressed, never purchase or gather lists of email addresses. This puts you in the same category as spammers and is not only really bad placement, but it is also against the law. In Chapter 6, we'll go into much more depth on placement.

Act like a person. Avoid composing emails in a robotic or professional letter-writing style. Email is a highly intimate medium, so write as if you were emailing a single individual, even if you are delivering the same message to thousands of subscribers. Go ahead and be a little casual.

Employ an email marketing service for businesses. Never utilize Gmail, Outlook, or any other common email provider for bulk email marketing purposes. These services are intended for individual emails, not bulk ones. If you use these services to send bulk emails, your account will be blocked or closed. There are user-friendly, reasonably-priced business email marketing platforms available. ConvertKit, MailChimp, Infusionsoft, Ontraport, and ActiveCampaign are a few well-known examples. The best part about utilizing these services is that they handle a lot of legal compliance automatically, such as including your contact information and an unsubscribe button at the bottom of your marketing letters. They also put a lot of effort into ensuring strong deliverability and eluding spam filters.

Email regularly. They will get "cold" if you don't send emails to your email database often. Even if they voluntarily subscribe to your email list, if they don't hear from you in a while, they can forget who you are and report you as a spammer. Even worse, your most valuable internet marketing asset begins to lose value. At a minimum, communicate with your email subscribers once a month to maintain a cordial connection. Weekly is more of a best practice; however, it also depends on who your target market is. There are email marketers that I know that send emails once a day, or perhaps more than once. Regarding frequency, there are no strict guidelines. Just make sure your email is valuable and relevant while sending it.

Give them something worthwhile. Your subscriber database will rapidly get weary of you sending them emails just when you want to sell them something, and they will either designate you as a spammer, unsubscribe from your list or ignore your emails. The foundation of any happy relationship is a value exchange. Make sure the bulk of your emails are informative content that adds value for your readers rather than sales pitches. Three emails that provide value for every email that makes an offer is a decent ratio.

Put in motion. Another wonderful incentive to utilize a professional email marketing platform is automation. With these platforms, you can create sequences that

automatically be sent to new subscribers via email. For instance, you could program your email marketing software to send them a welcome email immediately as soon as they enroll. After a day, it could send them an informative email that clarifies the product category they're interested in. It could send them an email with further information about you and your company three days later. You can ask them to arrange a call with you a week later. It is possible to automate all of this. Among your company's greatest salesmen may be your email marketing platform. It will always remember to follow up, never take a sick day, and never complain.

There are three difficulties with email marketing:

1. Sending and receiving emails. As was said, using a professional email marketing platform is the best method to guarantee strong email deliverability. Additionally, make sure that the email text you employ doesn't include too many photos, links, or spammy terms in it.

2. Getting responses to your emails. Having an attention-grabbing subject line is the best way to get your email opened. Headlines and copywriting strategies were covered in Chapter

2's copywriting section. Picture your email in the inbox of a prospect, one among hundreds. Your email subject line should pique the recipient's interest and encourage them to open your message.

3. Having an email read. Some marketers recommend sending brief emails to subscribers. The quality and relevancy of your emails matter more than their length. Your writing will be read if it is interesting. For instance, several well-known bloggers and email marketers compose lengthy emails. They also send regular emails to their subscribers. They know precisely what their target consumers want to read since they have gathered a wealth of data about them. Their emails are thus very intriguing and relevant to their target consumers, despite their length. Another strategy is to limit the length of emails to only having

a teaser or summary in the email body. The next step is to urge readers to visit your website or blog and read more by clicking on a link.

Email is an extremely effective and private media platform. It gives you the ability to highly automate the creation of engaging campaigns. It may be a useful component of an offline and online media strategy when executed properly.

Snail Mail

Many people believe that postal mail, sometimes known as "snail mail," is almost extinct in our day and age since social media, email, and the Internet play such major roles in our personal and professional connections. There is nothing more false than this.

I have a strong technological background and have used the Internet since the early days of dial-up. In addition, I co-founded two very successful software firms, which I assisted in growing from the ground up to a quick exit. Nevertheless, despite this history—or maybe even because of it—I consider "snail mail" to be among the most significant and underappreciated types of advertising media. It's important to realize that email is a supplement to postal mail when it comes to your media strategy.

Though we like the speed and effectiveness of everything digital, we would be remiss to undervalue the ability of real things to evoke strong feelings in others. And the main goal of marketing is to emotionally persuade consumers to take a desired action. Consider the difference between a husband telling his wife, "I love you," by text or email on their anniversary, and the same message sent on a handmade card accompanied by a bouquet of her favorite flowers. The physical and virtual versions of the same communication vary greatly from one another.

Have you ever gotten a postcard with a Google AdWords discount in the mail? The fact that Google, the digital era's poster child, incorporates postal mail into its small company marketing plan is instructive. Postal mail has to be disposed of with effort and has a significantly longer lifetime. Postal letters from important people in one's life are often treasured and kept for decades. Emails are temporary; they might be in your inbox one minute, erased, and then forgotten. This is seldom the case with other digital communications.

A further noteworthy aspect of postal mail is that it has drastically decreased clutter in recent years, which is a dream come true for marketers. The media has grown less crowded, which makes it even more attractive. Clutter is the enemy of message breakthrough. On the other hand, email has significantly increased clutter. Even proficient email sorters approach email with a whole different mindset than they do snail mail due to the absurd volume of noise that has crept into inboxes. When handling email, people linger their fingers above the delete key. Anything that isn't used right away is either archived in an inbox or removed, forwarded, or forgotten.

We are dependent on couriers and the postal service to move postal mail and physical items for us until we find out how to teleport them from one place to another as they do on Star Trek.

Postal mail is unquestionably an effective media outlet. Like with other media, it's crucial to avoid being fixated on or dependent on a particular channel. Whether you choose to use direct mail or another medium, your objective is to determine the best way to recoup your investment in media.

How to Invest in Marketing with No End

Without talking about the budget, no debate on marketing or media expenditures can be considered comprehensive. Whenever money is spent on marketing, one of three things will happen:

1. Your marketing is unsuccessful (that is, you earn less money from marketing than you invested).

2. Because you don't track the outcomes, you have no clue whether your marketing was successful or unsuccessful.

3. Your marketing is successful, or you generate a higher profit than you invested in it.

There is a straightforward course of action for each of these situations:

1. If your marketing continually backfires and costs you money, stop and make a change in strategy.

2. It's just dumb to not monitor your marketing outcomes since it's now easier than ever to track your ROI and marketing success thanks to widely and affordably accessible technologies.

3. You should step it up and put as much money into it as possible if your marketing is effective and regularly provides you with a favorable return on investment.

I find that one of the most absurd things small company owners do is create a "marketing budget." By establishing a marketing budget, you are essentially saying that your advertising is a waste of money or that it isn't working. Alternatively, you can't tell whether it's effective since you don't track the outcomes; instead, you just toss money at it in the hopes of seeing some kind of return. If the former is true, you must naturally create a budget, as you cannot have ongoing spending.

crazy in your line of work. However, you may want to consider why you are squandering money on ineffective marketing. Should the latter be true, you must act quickly to make changes. Just as you wouldn't hire a worker without tracking their output, why in the world would you continuously spend money on marketing without understanding the outcome it's producing?

You are getting a great return on investment from your marketing, so why in the world would you restrict it with a budget? Marketing that works is like owning a legitimate money-printing machine. We refer to this situation as "money at a discount." Would you not purchase as many $100 notes as you could if I were offering them for $80? Or would you say something like, "I'm sorry, but this month I only have $800 for discounted $100 bills? Please take ten."

That's why I always advise having an endless budget for effective marketing. One argument against this that I hear is that there may not be enough resources to meet the demand. First of all, it's a very good issue to have. Second, this is the ideal time to increase your pricing if you're getting more demand than you can meet. Your margins will increase immediately, and you'll attract higher-quality clients as a result.

Setting a marketing budget is only appropriate during the testing stage. I suggest you fail cheaply and often throughout the testing phase until you find a winner. Test the placement of your advertisement, the title, the offer, and other elements. Once you've found a combination that offers you the most return on investment, reduce the losers and maximize the winners.

Keep in mind that the post office bills you the same price for mailing a poor-quality direct mail piece that fails as they do for a high-converting item that brings in millions of dollars. Increase your marketing budget and, thus, the pace of your legal money printing machine, as soon as you have a winner that brings in more money than it costs!

The Number That Is The Most Dangerous

In your company, one is the most deadly number. It brittles companies.

Is there a single lead source for your company? A single, significant supplier? One significant client? Utilize only one kind of media. Provide only one kind of merchandise. Is there, to use a phrase from computer systems, "a single point of failure" in your company? If this is the case, your company is fragile, and even a little alteration in conditions outside your control might have disastrous consequences.

It's a pretty difficult circumstance to find yourself in. On the day when Google altered its search engine algorithm, several companies suffered greatly. These companies focused all of their marketing funds and efforts on search engine optimization and very immediately discovered that their only source of leads had vanished.

Similar to this, marketers that were paying Google huge sums of money every month suffered the "Google Slap" when the search engine began to alter the kinds of sponsored ads it wanted to display. In other words, Google began charging customers four, five, and sometimes even 10 times as much as they were charging them before. Advertisers were obliged by this adjustment to halt their campaigns and attempt to resolve the problem or locate other lead sources. Meanwhile, business as usual essentially came to an end. In the United States, fax broadcasting was essentially banned, and several companies that depended solely on it for lead generation failed.

Antiquity's wise teachings advise us to construct our home on a rock mass rather than sand. That way, our home won't collapse during the inevitable storm. Finding any situations where the number one might harm you is the first step. Here are a few instances: What would happen if your biggest client went out of business or defected to a rival? What happens if government regulations change and the product you now sell is banned or rendered completely obsolete? What happens if your primary marketing plan fails? What happens if your advertising expenses skyrocket? What would happen if your present high search engine rankings vanished or if your cost per click increased significantly? What happens if your largest supplier has a scarcity of supplies, increases pricing, or closes down? What would happen if the government were to push down even harder on email marketing?

These situations are all possible and do occur. You are essentially building your home on sand if you depend only on one thing. Relying on just one item leaves you vulnerable. The home will crumble when the storm arrives and the rivers rise. Find and remove the single points of failure in your company.

That way, your organization will be protected if rules change, advertising costs increase, or one particular technique suddenly loses its effectiveness. Since you are independent of everyone or anything, you will be the one in charge. Jim Rohn has a great theory on it: you have to consider winter in the summer. When the clouds are fluffy and the sky is blue, it's simply too simple to pull a practical joke. Winter will arrive; you must be ready for it every year.

Even if none of these outcomes materialize in the meantime, at least you will have established a more robust and valued company.

When it comes to media strategy, I often see that many small companies rely only on one source for new business. I recommend obtaining leads and clients from a minimum of five distinct sources. In addition, I advise using paid media for the majority of these five sources. Stated differently,

It costs you money to promote yourself to them. Paid media is significant for two reasons.

To start with, it is quite dependable. There's a very good chance my advertisement will be printed if I pay a newspaper to publish it. Gaining such a steady and dependable supply of leads via free, or ostensibly free, marketing strategies like word-of-mouth referrals is much more difficult.

Second, you are forced to consider return on investment (ROI) when using sponsored marketing. Cut a paid marketing strategy if it's not effective. You should stop wasting money or time on it. On the other hand, when we adopt an ostensibly free marketing strategy, like word-of-mouth advertising, we are often less efficient and waste a lot of time since there is no upfront cost. But there's also an opportunity cost that, upon further examination, often adds up to a startlingly substantial sum of actual cash.

The ability to reliably convert one dollar of paid advertising into one or more dollars in earnings via direct response marketing is both an art and a science that can help you accelerate business development and build a robust company.

Act II: The Part "During"

CHAPTER 4: GATHERING INQUIRIES

GATHERING INQUIRIES

Imagine that you are a hunter. After getting up in the morning and gathering your weapons, you go on the hunt. On some days, your family enjoys a feast when you return with a kill. On other days, your family goes without food, and you return empty-handed. It's a daily struggle to hunt successfully—the pressure is on all the time.

Consider yourself a farmer now. You sow your seeds and bide your time until they are ready to be harvested. You tend to them and provide for them in the meantime. You take care of and water your crop. When they're prepared, harvesting begins. I've found that most companies are hunters rather than farmers. Their goal is to bring in new business via cold calling. They put a ton of time and effort into finding new clients, and they will stop at nothing to get the deal done quickly. Their desperate attempts to compete on price and provide discounts in their advertising are evident in their hasty decision to close a deal. They annoy those who aren't interested in their goods or services for a ridiculous period.

The majority of company owners have no idea why they are promoting the way they are. They just put their company name, attractive logo, and a corny catchphrase about being the best in their field or sector in their advertisement. Most of them will respond to your question about the aim of their advertisement by saying

To "get their name out there" or to sell their goods is the goal. This is incorrect! Completely incorrect It would be as if they were throwing money down the drain.

Instead of attempting to close a deal right away, the goal of direct response marketing is to locate individuals who are interested in what you do. You add interested leads who reply to your follow-up database so you can establish credibility, provide value, and foster a connection based on trust.

If this is the appropriate thing for them to do, the sale follows naturally. Although it will need a mental adjustment, this is an idea that cannot be overlooked.

Why not try reaching them with your advertisement? Even if they are interested in what you do, the majority of individuals who read your advertisement won't be prepared to purchase on the same day that they see it. Some readers may indeed be ready to buy right away.

You will lose them if you do not enter them into a database. In a month, six months, or a year, they may have been available for purchase. However, because your advertisement was a "one-shot," you have thrown away that chance entirely. It is quite unlikely that they would recall your one-shot advertisement from half a year ago.

Marketing in this manner is like planting seeds in a field.

Using an Ethical Bribe to Extract Gold

It is not appropriate to treat every prospect identically, even in a small target market.

If everything else is equal, your odds of turning a high-probability prospect into a client are higher the more money you can spend on marketing to them.

Do you recall the archer we spoke about in Chapter 1? He only has so many arrows, just like you only have so much money to spend on your marketing campaign, so you have to be smart about how you use it.

For instance, you are effectively paying $1 for each prospect if you have $1,000 to spend on an advertising campaign that reaches 1,000 individuals.

Assume, for the moment, that 100 of the 1,000 individuals the advertisement touches are potential customers. You would be squandering $900 on indifferent and unenthusiastic prospects to reach the 100 who are interested if you treated them equally, which is what mass marketing would require.

What if you could filter, sort, and screen prospects rather than treat them all equally, allowing you to interact with just high-probability prospects and avoid spending time and money on disinterested and unmotivated ones?

The remaining $1,000 might then be allocated to the 100 high-probability prospects. Instead of having to spend a pitiful $1 on each prospect, if you treated them all equally, you could spend $10 courting each of them.

Do you believe our conversion rate would be higher if we had 10 times the firepower directed at the appropriate targets? Of course.

However, how can we distinguish the wheat from the chaff? We buy them out to inform us, is the succinct response!

We give an "ethical bribe" to persuade people to identify themselves with us, but don't worry, this isn't a dirty trick. As an example, our buddy the

A wedding photographer might provide a complimentary DVD that lists all the qualities a potential bride should look for in a wedding photographer and includes samples of his work.

A very basic advertisement to generate leads may say, "Free DVD Exposes the Seven Expensive Errors to Prevent When Selecting a Wedding Day Photographer."

Requesters of this "ethical bribe" would be indicating that they are a high-risk candidate. At a minimum, you now know their address and name, which you can add to your marketing database.

Recall that the main objective is to produce leads. Refrain from attempting to close deals with your advertisement. You just want to filter out the indifferent and unenthusiastic at this early stage so that you can compile a database of high-probability prospects.

The second major reason you should refrain from making a straight sale from your advertisement is that, on average, only 3% of your target market is highly motivated and prepared to purchase right away. Most mass marketing aims to convert these prospects. Nevertheless, another 7% are extremely willing to purchase, and another 30% are interested but not at this time. The remaining 30% are uninterested, and even if your goods were free, the last 30% would not accept them.

If you attempted to close deals straight from your advertisement, you would miss out on 97% of potential customers and only target the 3% who are prepared to purchase now.

Your addressable market grows to 40% when you create an ad that generates leads. To do this, you need to capture the 3% of potential customers who are ready to purchase today, in addition to the 7% who are amenable to a discussion and the 30% who are interested but not at this time.

Your advertising will be 1,233% more successful if you increase the addressable market from 3% to 40%.

There is an additional unintended consequence for those who are prepared to make an instant purchase. They see that you're not in a rush to offload or minimize your

item or service. They see that you are not simply going for the kill to close a deal, but also that you are interested in developing a connection first. Marketing in this way is like planting seeds on a farm. It's an investment in your future since your company and outcomes will increase along with the number of interested prospects in your database.

You gain credibility and authority when you instruct and educate others. You are obeyed and seen as having a sincere, helpful interest in other people instead of being questioned.

A typical campaign may include a free report or video series that aims to educate your prospect on what to look for, how to avoid being taken advantage of, and other important topics. You have fulfilled every promise in your marketing once your prospect obtains the whole information.

Your reputation for reliability soars. You're positioned as the expert and set aside from your competitors. There isn't any sales pressure in your advertisement to close a deal right away. Rather, you have started the process of asking potential customers to raise their hands. When they get in touch with you, as you request, they have shown you that they are high-probability prospects.

Handling Your Treasure

As a youngster, I loved to watch the futuristic cartoon The Jetsons. I was certain that we would all be flying automobiles by the time I grew up. Even after many years, my wife still believes that I haven't grown up, even though my major mode of transportation is still land-based.

Although contemporary automobiles come equipped with some attractive bells and whistles, the fundamental design and functionality of cars haven't altered much in over a century. That raises the issue, though: Why don't we all fly about in our aircraft?

Technology for personal flying has been available for a while and is surprisingly inexpensive. It would undoubtedly cost about the same in mass manufacturing as vehicles. What, then, is the issue? The quick answer is that personal flying is not supported by any infrastructure. Our infrastructure is based mostly on automobiles. Contemporary towns, homes, and structures are all designed to fit automobiles.

Why do some firms fail to obtain any leads or prospects, while others get a steady stream of them? Infrastructure is the solution, just as it is to our flying problems.

A marketing infrastructure that consistently generates new leads, follows up with them, nurtures them, and turns them into devoted customers is what some companies have constructed. Some firms—indeed, most businesses, in my opinion—engage in what I refer to as "random acts of marketing." They post advertisements wherever they go, maybe on a brochure or website. They are not constructing a system in which a cold lead enters one end and a devoted consumer exits the other.

These intermittent, one-time, haphazard marketing initiatives often result in more expenses than revenues, which is discouraging and sometimes leads to

to make absurd statements to company owners, such as "Marketing doesn't work in my industry."

We must plan a system from beginning to finish to construct it. We must comprehend its operation and the resources required to operate it.

Your database of clients and prospects is a vital component of your marketing infrastructure, but to handle it efficiently, a customer relationship management (CRM) system is a must. The hub of your marketing operations is the CRM system. That's where your goldmine is managed.

All of your leads and interactions with customers should be recorded in your CRM. Things become interesting at this point.

CHAPTER 5: DEVELOPING PROSPECTS

DEVELOPING PROSPECTS

The World's Greatest Salesman's Secret

Joe Girard has the title of "the world's greatest salesman," according to Guinness World Records. He has, one by one, sold more expensive retail merchandise than any other salesman in history. Was he marketing some incredible new gadget that was a must-have for everyone? No. Was he catering to the ultra-wealthy? Again, incorrect. He sold regular automobiles to regular folks. Between 1963 and 1978, he sold nearly 13,000 automobiles at a Chevrolet dealership. His numbers are astounding. He sold 13,001 automobiles in all. That's an average of six automobiles every day. He sold eighteen cars on one of his greatest days. In his finest month, 174 were sold. His finest year's sales totaled $1,425. By himself, Joe Girard sold more automobiles than ninety-five percent of dealerships in North America. He sold them at retail, one car at a time, which made his accomplishment even more amazing. No fleet trades in bulk.

What was Joe's success formula? He mentions a few, such as putting forth a lot of effort and being likable. Without taking into account these other considerations, I'm confident that hundreds of salespeople at the time had similar commendable traits, but their number of sales was much less than Joe's. Joe's habit of being in continual communication with his clients was one of his most notable actions. Every month, he sent a handwritten greeting card to every client on his list.

It would be a Happy New Year card with the words "I like you" inside in January. Subsequently, he would affix his signature and provide the dealership's data. His list may get a Valentine's Day card in February. The identical message was included once more: "I like you."

Each envelope was hand-addressed and stamped, and he would alter its color and size. This was essential to avoiding the postal mail version of spam filters when individuals pick over the trash can and throw out anything that seems to be spam, such as credit card offers, advertisements, or other junk mail. His goal was for his clients to feel good when they opened his package, saw his name, and read the encouraging message inside. He knew they would soon need a new automobile, so he continued doing this month after month, year after year. Who do you suppose would have been at the forefront of their minds when they did? By the time his career was coming to an end, he was sending out 13,000 cards a month and needed an assistant.

Almost two-thirds of his sales were to returning clients by the time he had been in business for ten years. Customers were forced to schedule appointments in advance to visit and make purchases from him. Contrast that with other auto salesmen who waited about waiting and hoping for walk-in traffic.

Selling Like a Farmer

How often do salespeople follow up on leads on average, in your opinion? You would be about right if you made one or two guesses.

A full 50% of salesmen quit after only one contact, 65% quit after two, and 79.8% quit after three attempts. 1 What if a farmer sowed seeds but didn't give them any more than a single or double watering? Would his crop be a success? Not really.

The follow-up is where the money is in marketing. Based on this, we created the irresistible lead nurturing model.

A lead should be entered into your system as soon as it is obtained and should be followed up with throughout time. Making contact does not include aggressively pressuring prospects to make a purchase. By providing them with value before they purchase anything from you, you establish a rapport with them, earn their confidence, and establish your authority in your area of expertise.

Recognize that the majority of consumers won't be prepared to purchase now. Place them in a database, which should ideally record both email and physical direct mail information. Send them something every so often to keep in contact and establish yourself as a subject-matter expert in your business or profession (more on that in the next chapter).

You prepare your prospects to be ready for harvesting, much like a farmer. Like Joe Girard, you too can amass a large pipeline of prospective clients who will think of you first when they're ready to make a purchase. What's even more thrilling is that the value you've produced in advance will have already made them want to work with you. It won't take much persuasion or forced selling; the sale will naturally come up next.

The most significant asset in your company will be the relationships you have with the people on this increasing list of prospects. The golden goose is that. Rather than being a bother, you are an invited visitor who is welcomed when the prospect is finally ready to purchase. Becoming a marketing farmer is the most crucial lesson to learn from this message. It's an easy, three-step procedure:

1. Run advertisements to attract individuals who share your interests. Offer a free report, video, audio interview, and so on to do this. Any kind of pertinent, freely available information that offers a fix for an issue they're having will do. By doing this, you present yourself less as a marketer and more as an authority and educator. Which vendor would you rather purchase from?

2. Include them in the database.

3. Take care of them consistently and provide them with useful information, for instance, a newsletter about your sector or tips on maximizing the benefits of whatever you do or supply. Crucial advice: Don't turn this into an ongoing sales pitch. That will go stale pretty fast. Make sure you provide them with insightful content along with the odd pitch or exclusive deal. Primarily, remember to stay in touch; if you don't, the prospect will forget you and your connection will become that of a cold prospect and pest salesman.

As your database expands in size and quality, you will reap rich and continuous rewards if you become a "marketing farmer."

Developing Your Infrastructure for Marketing

We covered the idea of advertising to generate leads in the last chapter. Finding leads is one thing, but what truly sets the boys apart from the men—so to speak—is what you do with them. Have you ever contacted a company to inquire about a product or service and never heard back? Or maybe, after getting a quotation, all you got was a sloppily worded follow-up call? This indicates a malfunctioning marketing infrastructure.

The unfortunate part is that a CRM system can automate much, if not all, of the tedious follow-up labor. The majority of reliable CRM systems may be configured to send a customer an email or SMS automatically or to notify a salesperson to follow up with a call. The automation may be started by a pre-set timer, by monitoring inquiries and purchases, or by a response from the prospect. To make better use of your time, automation technologies enable you to automatically sort, filter, and screen leads and clients.

You have a database of high-probability prospects now; your task is to keep promoting them until they either purchase or pass away. It can seem like I'm supporting being pushy and hounding them until they give in. There is nothing more false than this.

Conventional sales training often emphasizes clumsy little pressure-based close strategies like "always be closing" and other similar approaches. The salesperson becomes a nuisance that the potential customer wants to stay away from.

I suggest being a welcomed visitor rather than a bothersome one. Provide a steady stream of value to your high-probability prospects until they're prepared to make a purchase. This might take the form of guides, papers, case studies, or even something as basic as a newsletter that is released every month and pertains to their field of interest. By doing this, you establish rapport and trust and present yourself as an authority and teacher rather than simply a pushy salesperson.

This ongoing follow-up process may be easily automated with a variety of technological solutions, which makes it a scalable and reasonably priced method of accumulating a large pipeline of motivated and interested leads.

While some of these prospects may become clients right away, others may take weeks, months, or even years to do so. The key is that you should have established a strong rapport with them based on trust and value by the time they're ready to make a purchase. When the time comes for them to decide what to purchase, you will be the obvious option because of this.

Because it is entirely based on trust and value exchange, this is one of the most moral and easy methods to sell. With this method, you are concentrating all of your firepower on a single, easily identifiable target, while your rivals are aimlessly firing arrows in every direction in the hopes of striking one of the 3% of instant purchasers.

The "assets" that make up your marketing infrastructure will include A few of the resources I've effectively implemented in marketing infrastructures that I've created or assisted in overseeing are listed below: websites that collect leads Freely recorded message information lines Newsletters Blogs No-cost reports Sequences for direct mail email chains Social networks DVDs and videos on the internet Audio CDs and podcasts Print advertisements written by hand Autoresponders for emails Auto-responders for SMS Shock and awe bundles (covered in the section after this one)

All of them are part of my marketing infrastructure. I'm still working on larger, more complex items, but these are some of the foundational pieces. There is a place and a purpose for each of them. Every advertisement I run is intended to feed cold leads into this system and turn them into devoted followers.

Of course, creating a marketing infrastructure like this requires resources, but much like creating a physical infrastructure like a road or train system, the majority of the time and money is spent on the initial construction. It's merely maintenance and continuous improvement after that.

The interesting part is that a large portion of my marketing strategy is automated now that technology has advanced, giving me a lot of power. Once I've found a mixture that works, I can use it again with consistent outcomes.

My outcomes get better as I keep expanding my marketing infrastructure. How about you? Are you constructing the foundation for your marketing? Are your marketing systems being enhanced and improved regularly?

If you accomplish this, you'll have a significant advantage over your rivals, who will just be fumbling about with sporadic marketing campaigns.

The Shock and Awe Package and Lumpy Mail

We covered the effectiveness of postal mail as a media channel in Chapter 3. One method to give this potent media outlet a boost is via "lumpy mail." Consider how you typically categorize mail. One day, you discover something lumpy inside one of the envelopes in your collection of envelopes. It contains a 3D tangible item, maybe a book, DVD, or other trinket. Which of your envelopes will get the most attention and be opened first? It will be the lumpy one if you're typical.

Lumpy mail draws attention and gives you a lot of creative freedom when designing direct mail pieces. "Grabbers" are the term used in the direct mail business to describe little items that are intentionally placed to draw attention. Typically, grabbers establish the tone for your sales message. For instance, if the sales letter's topic is "Stop Wasting Money," you may include a little plastic garbage can inside the envelope. Alternatively, you might place a magnet inside that says, "Attract More Clients." It may seem cheesy, and it most likely is, but when done well, it draws attention, amuses, and, most importantly, produces excellent outcomes.

You may even stuff books, CDs, and DVDs into envelopes to give them a lumpy appearance. These things usually don't get thrown away, except for drawing attention when they are opened. What you send will probably be kept by your clients and potential clients forever, serving as a continual reminder of who you are.

The "shock and awe package" elevates lumpy mail to a new level. 2 Possibly one of the most effective follow-up techniques for direct response marketing that is now available in the "shock and awe" bundle. When done correctly, it may propel conversions to new heights and elevate your brand far above rivals. It's so strong that it almost destroys your rivals and places you in a league of its own. Shock and awe packages have such amazing quality that even when your

When rivals learn what you're doing, they often won't dare try to replicate it. Almost nobody engages in this.

We spoke about how important it is to record the information of prospects who have shown interest in the last chapter. Naturally, the goal of this is to stay in contact with them and develop a relationship with them until the time comes for them to become clients.

Now recall the last time you made a product- or service-related inquiry. Maybe you sent us an email, called, or used a website to submit your query. You performed the standard "send me more information" dance. In answer to this inquiry, what did you receive? Most likely, the company you contacted took one of the following actions: I sent you a URL for a page. I sent you an email, maybe with a few attachments. addressed your questions throughout our phone conversation.

They may have followed any or all of the foregoing advice. Observe what's taking place. They're answering your question as economically and effectively as possible. While being inexpensive and effective has its merits, nobody will find it inspiring, thrilling, or amusing. Nobody is going to pause and exclaim, "Wow, I received a PDF file with all the specs." How fantastic!

One of the following three impressions might be formed in the first exchanges you have with prospects:

1. identical

2. shoddy

3. breathtakingly incredible

The majority of company owners choose option 1, a surprisingly high proportion select option 2, and almost none select option 3. It's up to you to figure out how to be option 3. Thankfully, there's no need to start from scratch. Using a "shock and awe package" is one of the finest methods to wow someone beyond belief.

Essentially, a shock and awe package is a tangible box that you send or present to potential customers that is filled with special, highly advantageous resources associated with your company and sector. A shock-and-awe package should include the following items, to name a few: Books: individuals are socialized to hardly ever discard books. If it's a book you authored, major extra points. Books are a powerful tool for promoting yourself; they can suddenly transform you from a salesman to a knowledgeable authority and educator. With this book, I'm doing this right now! discs or DVDs that introduce you and the particular issues your company, service, or product resolves for your potential client. Testimonials from prior customers in video, audio, or written form. snippets of articles or pieces in the media regarding you, your business, or your goods sales letters, brochures, and other marketing materials White papers or independent studies that support your position or highlight the benefits of the kind of product or service you provide. a demonstration of your goods or services. Face value Coupons or gift cards may have a lot of sway since it seems like "wasting money" to toss them away. These encourage the potential client to give you a try. Unusual trinkets and presents that amuse, instruct, and amaze. I've heard of everything being offered, even iPads and customized coffee cups. Handwritten messages thanking them for enquiring or rehashing a discussion you've had with them over the phone.

What the heck? I hear you utter. In this instantaneous, on-demand "information age," snail mail? Yes, that is the response! I promise you that no one likes technology as much as I do. I'm always addicted to one of several screens, and I'm a sucker for the newest "anything." But like most people, I like getting packages, and it's much more exciting when they arrive unexpectedly.

Even though individuals used to send out a lot more snail mail, it's now simpler than ever to intercept physical mail, particularly parcels. How long does it take you to tear open a FedEx package if it falls on your desk? It's probably not that lengthy if you're like most people.

I'm not suggesting you shouldn't reply to information requests by phone, email, or the Internet right away, but you should be aware that the first exchanges with a potential customer are crucial and should be handled with great care. Nothing ought to rely just on luck. A fantastic tool for making your prospect say "wow" is a shock and awe bundle.

Three goals should be achieved by a shock-and-awe package: Offer your prospect remarkable, unexpected value. Present yourself as a knowledgeable and reliable authority in your industry. Get your prospect to go further down the purchasing cycle than they otherwise would have.

This is much more effective than the typical response of "Sure, I'll shoot you an email with more information."

The claim that shock-and-awe packages are excessively costly is a frequent criticism of them. As we covered in the last chapter, your odds of converting high-probability prospects to customers increase with the amount of money you can spend on marketing to them. That is the main purpose of the shock and awe pack. You'll blow them away if you can outspend your rival in courting and impressing potential customers. Of course, if you don't know your metrics, especially ones like client lifetime value, you'll lose money. Poor arithmetic cannot be compensated for with effective marketing.

Of course, the numbers have to add up. If your firm is solely transactional and has very low margins, which is something I strongly advise against, the numbers should add up, and delivering the shock-and-awe package should be quite cost-effective.

When it comes to courting potential customers, avoid the error of being economical and effective. Packages for shock and awe are quite competitive.

benefit. If rivals are like most firms, they won't know their figures, so the majority of them won't grasp them, and even those that do typically lack the guts to utilize them. They'll probably think they're too costly since there are more affordable and effective strategies to get clients. While your marketing wows, entertains, excites, and inspires, let your rivals perform inexpensive and effective advertising. You will be quite different after that.

Turn into a successful marketer.

High-growth companies often spend substantially on marketing and make a lot of offers. This is one of their similarities. While some of these offers prove to be blockbusters, others prove to be flops. The interesting aspect is that, particularly if you start by testing with a tiny portion of your list, you don't need many hits to make up for your misses.

You begin to have a clear understanding of what works and what doesn't by making a lot of offers. As a marketer gains volume, it becomes much simpler to identify patterns and use split testing to assess reactions objectively.

A crucial characteristic of rapidly expanding companies is their willingness to take risks with their proposals. They take chances, use persuasive language, and make outlandish claims.

Is that all there is to it? Developing more attractive and regular offers? Well, to put it simply, yeah. The principles are constant. The foundations remain the same, even if there are additional media channels to use for offers and new marketing technologies to measure ROI and do split tests.

Faster company growth is the result of more frequent and appealing offerings.

Increasing the frequency of your marketing will generate excitement inside your company. You will become more noticeable to your customers and prospects, break through the noise, and increase the volume of sales coming into your funnel.

Positive or bad, every alteration that gets ingrained in your habit will eventually have a significant effect. You'll quickly notice a significant change in your company if you include creating and distributing offers to your list of consumers and prospects in your daily routine.

Creating deals regularly helps improve your marketing. Gaining proficiency in the science of marketing is essential for quick company expansion. And things will get better for you once you recover.

Create It, Make It Happen, and Make It Continue

You were taught to be autonomous in school. To advance to the next level, you needed to pass science, math, and English. Let's say you combined your skills with those of a few pals. All of the math exams were completed by one math-proficient acquaintance. All the scientific examinations were completed by a second acquaintance who excelled in science. Since you were proficient in English, you completed all of the exams in that language. That kind of cooperative work arrangement would have been deemed cheating in the classroom, and the three of you might have faced consequences or maybe been expelled. However, in the corporate world, combining various skills to work toward a common objective is precisely the kind of organization that produces positive results. In the team sport of business, individual success is unattainable.

Different "types" are needed for a firm to succeed. The three main kinds are as follows:

1. The entrepreneur: sometimes known as the visionary or person of ideas. They are prepared to take chances to address

a problem or market gap and turn a profit. For instance, they fabricate it by identifying a need in the market for a certain product and recruiting the necessary personnel to launch the enterprise.

2. The specialist: this person carries out the idea of the business owner. They could be a graphic designer, an engineer, or a venture investor. They assist in bringing the vision—or at least a portion of it—to life. By constructing the facility to manufacture the product, optimizing the tools, and designing the product packaging, they bring it to life.

3. The manager: they ensure that tasks are completed, work is provided, and the goal is being pursued each day when they arrive. For instance, they keep it going by managing the manufacturing, ensuring that shipments are made on schedule, and ensuring that the quality is correct.

Business success requires all three categories, but it's quite uncommon for one individual to excel in all three. Rarely are small company owners managers; instead, they are often the experts, the entrepreneurs, or both.

Even if you run your company alone right now, you still need to figure out how to cover all three bases. You may hire someone or outsource this work. Small company owners sometimes attempt to take on too much, which leads to items unavoidably falling through the cracks. A marketing infrastructure often never gets up and running properly because there is no management position. That explains why there are never any shock and awe packages received or monthly newsletters. Although the company owner may agree that these are excellent ideas for lead nurturing—which they are—they are too busy to do the operational tasks without a manager overseeing the marketing infrastructure.

Therefore, if you don't regularly use advanced marketing assets and techniques like a shock and awe package, what use are they?

In many other areas of your company, all three jobs are most likely already covered. For instance, you made up the notion and vision for what you were going to develop when you first started. The legal framework of the company may then have been established by you hiring a lawyer; your lawyer gave it reality. Then, your accountant may arrange for you to have them handle your tax returns and compliance on an annual basis.

You must apply the same logic to your marketing infrastructure. Install systems (we cover them in greater detail in Chapter 7). Create the marketing concepts, or even better, take them straight out of this book; employ web developers, graphic designers, and copywriters to bring them to life; and finally, engage administrative assistants or fulfillment services to ensure that it happens again. Much of this can be mechanized, as was previously described, and what cannot be automated should be assigned. It's just too significant to ignore. A non-operational marketing infrastructure may be detrimental to your company, even fatal.

Because the government enforces your yearly tax responsibilities, probably, you don't ignore them. Their calendar sets deadlines for filing tax returns and paying different taxes.

With a "marketing calendar," you may create a forcing mechanism that is comparable. A marketing calendar outlines the necessary marketing activities on a daily, weekly, monthly, quarterly, and yearly basis. These are scheduled in the same manner as other significant business events.

For instance, you may determine that your company would benefit from the following marketing calendar: Every day, look for mentions on social media and reply suitably. Every week, publish a blog entry and provide email list subscribers with the link in a broadcast email. Send a printed newsletter or postcard to clients and potential clients once a month. Quarterly: Send a reactivation letter to previous clients who haven't purchased in a while. Every year, thank every client for their business by sending them a gift basket.

Once the tasks and deadlines have been determined, the only thing left to decide is who will be in charge of carrying out each of these planned marketing initiatives. Again, don't attempt to handle everything alone if you're a tiny business or lone proprietor. As much as feasible, assign someone else to do these monotonous operational tasks.

You should take into account event-triggered marketing initiatives in addition to your normal, planned marketing campaigns. Take these event triggers and their accompanying actions, for instance: When you run into a prospective customer at a networking event, enter their information from their business card into your CRM system and add them to your mailing list for your monthly email or postcard. When you get an incoming sales inquiry, deliver your shock and awe package along with a handwritten message. After your blog brings in a new email list subscriber, connect them to your CRM system and set up an automated five-part video series that will be sent to them over the following thirty days. You received a complaint from a customer. Please send them a handwritten apologetic letter and a $100 voucher for their next purchase after the problem has been remedied.

Again, assign as much responsibility as you can to these event-triggered tasks. This will free you up to work on more advanced marketing projects, including creating and evaluating fresh campaigns or enhancing the value of your product. Few company endeavors are as lucrative as improving your marketing.

Employ administrative support in the form of a manager to "run the factory" for you and ensure that your planned and event-triggered marketing efforts are carried out, even if your company is now tiny.

Being business owners, we have an optimistic outlook. This often implies that we are inclined to roll up our sleeves and get things done when they need to be done. But if you find yourself putting a lot of time into activities that aren't within your area of expertise or aren't a smart use of your time, it can easily turn into a costly exercise. Recall that, whereas time is a finite resource, money is a renewable resource that you can always get more of.

Quality is another frequent issue when it comes to outsourcing or work delegation. Will they do the task to the same standard as you? The likelihood is probably not. However, I prefer to follow the general rule of thumb that you should delegate something if someone else can do it 80% as well as you can.

It might be hard to let go, particularly if, like most entrepreneurs, you're a control freak and perfectionist. However, it's essential if you want your firm to have leverage and scalability. If not, you wind up giving up other things and paying yourself the minimum wage for repetitive labor.

high-value activities such as creating your marketing infrastructure, which may take your firm to a whole new level.

These timeless words of wisdom come from Jim Rohn:

Discover how to distinguish between majors and minors. Many individuals struggle just because they major in unimportant subjects.

Never confuse progress with accomplishment. It's easy to fool yourself by seeming busy. What are you busy doing, exactly?

Days cost a lot. You only have one day left after spending a day. So, make sure you spend each one carefully.

The same goes for modest time spent on important things as it does for significant time spent on tiny things.

Money is not as important as time. More money may be obtained, but more time cannot be obtained.

The wealthiest people's best-kept secret is time.

Lastly, the most frequent criticism is that hiring or outsourcing assistance is too costly. A few years ago, this could have been the case, but with the advent of geo arbitrage, it is no longer the case. Southeast Asia, India, and Eastern Europe have a vast talent pool of workers who will work for you for a fraction of the cost of hiring local workers and contractors.

Large corporations relocate much of their standard activities to these areas for a good reason. They are brimming with skilled, motivated, educated, and competent English-speaking laborers.

As you sleep, you may set up chores and have them appear out of nowhere. Significantly, scalability is equally as important as cost. When employing and discharging staff members or even contractors locally, you would have to follow a plethora of bureaucratic requirements. But with the help of enormous internet job platforms like 99Designs, Upwork, and Freelancer, you can employ a horde of

personal assistants, graphic designers, web developers, and practically any other talent you may think of. Any of these may be brought on board as permanent team members or recruited as needed for certain projects.

This book's creation is the ideal illustration of this. I wrote it in Australia, and two copyeditors—one from the US and the other from Canada—edited it. My research assistant was situated in the Philippines, while the cover design was created by a graphic artist in India. Geographical restrictions have been removed via the Internet, making it possible for anyone to operate globally. Never before has there been so much affordable and easily accessible talent.

Of course, others will always bring up the old, boring issue between local employment and patriotism, but how many jobs can you generate locally if you fail to use important marketing methods and go out of business? Talent and labor are globalized, and they have been for a while. International outsourcing and geo arbitrage, which were formerly exclusive to big, multinational corporations, are now easily accessible to small and medium-sized enterprises as well as individual entrepreneurs like you and me. This changes the game. Instead of fighting change, it is our responsibility as entrepreneurs to embrace it and figure out how to use it to our advantage.

As you become more prosperous, one of the benefits of your success will be the creation of local employment. You will be supporting your local community and generating employment locally when you update your home, make a large charitable donation, or purchase a new car—most of which would not be feasible if your firm collapses.

CHAPTER 6: CONVERSION OF SALES

CONVERSION OF SALES

You've certainly heard the cheesy old joke that occurs in the classic movie The Pink Panther Strikes Again. Playing the unfortunate Inspector Clouseau, Peter Sellers asks the guy standing next to an adorable puppy, "Does your dog bite?" in a horrible French accent. "No," the guy answers, shaking his head. The dog lashes out and bites Clouseau's hand as he reaches out to pat it. With a furious expression, he goes back to face the guy and demands, "I thought you said your dog didn't bite?" The guy says, "That's not my dog," in a nonchalant manner.

The folks you're marketing believe that all dogs bite because they have been bitten far too often. You're not even beginning the selling process on neutral ground—rather, you're starting behind in negative territory, unless you're the well-known incumbent in your field. Despite your ethical conduct, your prospects lack trust and are skeptical. Unfortunately, you have to gain their confidence and go from a bad to a positive area before making a sale since it's a case of guilty until proven innocent.

You need to have some effective techniques for sales conversion since trust is the main obstacle to a transaction. Although a whole sales training program is beyond the purview of this book, we will examine many ideas and approaches in this chapter that will greatly simplify the sales conversion process. 1 In particular, we'll talk about the pivotal function that

positioning and how to include appropriate positioning into your process for converting sales based on trust.

We discussed capturing and nurturing high-probability leads in the preceding two chapters to establish authority, value, and trust. The goal of all of this was to make the sales conversion process simple and natural. Prospects should be pre-framed, pre-motivated, pre-interested, and begging to purchase from you by the time they reach the sales conversion stage. You should probably enhance your lead nurturing procedure if you have to persuade them or make a strong pitch.

Most salespeople portray themselves as either needy beggars or arrogant, aggressive salespeople utilizing foolish outmoded "closing" tactics like ABC (always be closing), the trial close, or the assumptive close. In the world of sales, these methods are now considered ridiculous, and unless you're door-to-door selling low-value goods like vacuum cleaners, they will do more harm than good to your prospects.

Anticipating sales to occur simply as a result of the business's existence is another similarly poor strategy that many new firms adopt. Some create a website and hope that sales will come in naturally, while others develop a real shop. They use hope as a marketing tactic. Indeed, they may close a few deals just by chance, as when a prospect happens to walk by. However, that will only lead to frustration. Many of these companies sell just enough to enable people to kill themselves via torture. The market or their sector is too competitive, they decide.

In all honesty, I'm not aware of any market or business that lacks competition. However, I can say with certainty that, regardless of how competitive a market or business is, there will always be some success stories and unsuccessful stories.

To be completely honest with ourselves, we couldn't attribute it to a market or industry issue. What, then, is the issue? The issue is

Most likely, they are trying to market themselves as a commodity, a "me too" kind of company.

Your only marketing options when you position yourself this

way are to either drastically reduce your rates (which is risky) or yell as loudly as you can (which is extremely costly). You don't want pricing to be your primary difference unless you are a Costco, Walmart, or other massive company—that's an impossible war to win.

By now, a lot of these companies have realized their foolishness and are claiming to be "the best," "the highest quality," and other such claims that are questionable and hard to prove.

Nothing financial is in your goods or services.

The way you promote yourself will have a significant influence on the kind of customers you draw in and the price you can charge for your services, regardless of whether you're offering freshly made bread, accounting services, or IT help. A widely held misconception is that "it's all about the product," meaning that if you provide a superior-good or service, customers will always choose to do business with you and pay more for it.

While, to some degree, this is accurate, once your product or service reaches a "good enough" level, the law of diminishing returns kicks in. How much better than your competitors' bread, accountancy services, or IT assistance, after all? The real money, after you've attained a certain degree of proficiency, is in how you sell yourself.

What is the salary of a professional violinist? That will depend on how he promotes himself, however. Are you familiar with Joshua Bell? He is among the world's best classical musicians. He earns up to $1,000 every minute performing to sold-out crowds all around the globe. He performs on a 1713-built Stradivarius violin that is today worth $3.5 million. At over three centuries old, this particular Stradivarius violin is considered the most exquisitely-sounding instrument ever made.

Thus, we have the world's best violinist playing the most exquisite violin ever. Bell is without a doubt the greatest musician he has ever worked with. He was asked to take part in a sociological experiment by the Washington Post while his career was at its peak. They wanted him to perform for an hour at a nearby subway station, where he would be heard by thousands of passing pedestrians. Thus, with his violin case open, Bell performed a set list of classical classics early on January 12, 2007. How much did the world's best violinist, who plays a stunning $3.5 million violin, make in one hour? $32 in total.

The best violinist in the world, performing on the most exquisite instrument, received a pitiful $32 from his "clients." A few nights before, the same violinist performed at a Boston music venue for an audience that paid $100 or more per ticket. During that event, he made almost $60,000 every hour.

The same gifted artist, performing the same piece on the violin, may make $32 per hour in one situation and $60,000 in another. Why was there such a noticeable change? Simply put placement.

If you're a professional musician and you market yourself as a subway busker, you'll be treated and compensated appropriately by your "customers." On the other hand, if you market yourself as a professional concert musician, you draw in a whole other clientele and get compensated appropriately once again. Put another way, until you can demonstrate differently, people will usually accept you for who you are.

Of course, claiming to be a professional musician and then showing up unable to give a strong performance would be dishonest. It holds regardless of the kind of company you operate. What's keeping you from presenting your high-quality product or service at a much higher level, charging a premium for it, and drawing in a much better caliber of clientele?

Decide to no longer market yourself as a commodity and engage in price-only competition. Your bottom line will benefit greatly from this.

Changing from Pest to Valuable Guests

Regarding a close friend who arrives at your front door, how do you feel? Compare this to how you would feel if a stranger interrupted your family's meal or time spent together to sell things door to door. What makes a difference? The former is someone you know and have a relationship with; thus, you should welcome them as guests. The latter is bothersome. You don't even need or desire what he's selling, and you have no idea who he is or where he came from.

While the pest exists just to disturb and take, the welcoming visitor adds value to your life. Wouldn't it be wonderful to approach a potential customer and have them greet you as a valued visitor rather than as an annoyance? When a prospect is interested in what you have to offer and you are greeted with open arms, selling suddenly becomes simpler and more enjoyable. This is the change I want to see in your company and marketing strategy. Change from being an annoyance to a welcomed visitor.

Most companies attempt to sell without first building a rapport. They either use antiquated, ineffective means of advertising or make cold calls.

This is problematic since you're asking a potential consumer to decide on you before they've even had a chance to learn about your brand or values. They don't trust you yet; they don't like you, and they don't know you.

Like asking someone out on a first date, it could work once in a while, but is it something you want to risk everything on? You'll squander a lot of time, effort, and money on unqualified prospects, and you'll wind up with a subpar closing ratio of, say, one in ten or one in twenty. Furthermore, you'll squander a lot of cash on subpar advertising.

When someone calls you after seeing a generic advertisement

and you respond, "Sure, I can come out and see you," or "Sure, I can help you," the

The issue with this is that your conversion rate is probably far lower than it might be since they hardly know you and are probably simply looking for a deal.

At this point, a lot of entrepreneurs develop an addiction to the drug "hopeium." When you "think" you have a potential customer who is interested in you and gives you favorable signals but who isn't planning to purchase from you, hopeium, a "drug," enters your body and thoughts. When a potential customer asks you to "tell me more about your product," "send me a quote," or "send me more information," the drug is often triggered. I think you get what I mean. You get a "rush" of excitement when someone contacts your office and expresses interest in what you have to offer because you know this may be your next big sale.

Then, after pursuing them nonstop for a few days or weeks, you get the "silent treatment." They've shown interest in what you have to offer throughout several great chats, but all of a sudden nothing is said. Try giving them a call once or twice. Even after sending a follow-up email, nothing happens. They just vanish. You believe that you have lost the sale, but you are unsure of what went wrong with your product or what you did incorrectly. It gives the impression that selling is a really difficult and unpleasant procedure.

Because hopeium isn't grounded in the reality of your prospect's true thoughts, it might be harmful. You'll stop spending selling time pursuing prospects who aren't a real match for your solution the sooner you "detox" from Hopeium.

Prospects have become more doubtful over time. They just don't trust you because they have been burned too many times. The issue is that you are beginning in negative territory rather than at zero. Furthermore, the traditional "close, close, close... sell, sell, sell..." strategy is no longer effective. Because they don't trust you, potential clients back down and do nothing.

Rather, you need to adopt the "educate, educate, educate" paradigm. Education helps you develop your trust. You may establish your expertise by getting an education. Education facilitates connection-building. Education facilitates the selling process for both the buyer and the seller.

As we covered in the last chapter, the first thing you do is provide your readers with something of value that informs them about a problem they have, rather than attempting to sell it to them right away. You may utilize a lot of free instructional resources, such as online webinars, audio interviews, videos, reports, and more.

Postponing the transaction serves two purposes. It first dismantles sales resistance by demonstrating your willingness to offer long before you take. Secondly, it showcases you as an authority in your domain and an instructor. Consider it. Which would you rather purchase from—a pushy salesman eager for their next commission or a knowledgeable instructor who cares about your needs and wants to assist you in solving your problem?

You need to stop selling and begin informing, counseling, and counseling potential customers about the advantages your goods and services provide over those of every other company in your industry.

You should read it again since it could be really valuable to you.

It's a fact that nobody likes to be seen as the standard aggressive, unreliable salesman. But I'm sure you'll feel much more at ease selling in such situations if you see yourself as a doctor who first diagnoses patients' issues and then recommends remedies —that is, as a reliable, informed, qualified, self-assured, and competent counselor.

And that's just what you want to come across to potential clients as—someone who can help them learn and find solutions to their issues.

I'd like to use this opportunity to explain to you what I mean when I say that an entrepreneur is "someone who solves people's problems at a profit."

In summary, never even give them the impression that you are a salesperson. Consultative selling via a nurturing system is the most effective approach to doing all of this (more on that in a moment). You have to think of yourself as a change agent who adds significant value, advantages, and benefits to the lives of your clients and potential clients.

Become the foremost authority in your field or business. To be honest, everyone thinks they are an expert; their marketing simply stinks. The coffee shop does a terrible job of publicizing the fact that it makes the greatest coffee.

The most economical, long-lasting, significant, and potent marketing tactic a company owner could ever create is consultative, advice-selling.

As long as you decide to counsel, consult, and inform potential customers or clients about the advantages your product offers, you have the upper hand at this point. In the chaotic society we live in today, it's the only way to reclaim the buyer's authority. Thus, give up selling and begin giving advice and education. Both your bank manager and your customers will value you more as a result.

Producing Confidence

Most individuals will tell you that they hate doing business with big, stupid firms. Large corporations are often characterized by poor service, apathetic workers, and out-of-touch management. Nevertheless, knowing that there are certainly much better solutions available, we continue to deal with them for some reason.

This is mostly due to the consolation that, even if the experience may not be ideal, it probably won't be awful. "Better the devil you know than the devil you don't," as the adage goes. Many consumers automatically dislike small enterprises because of scammers and those who seem to be fly-by-night entrepreneurs. Individuals are aware that while a big business may not provide the finest service, they are not likely to be deceived by them directly.

Running a small company immediately puts you at a disadvantage. A consumer who thoroughly investigates you may find that you are reliable and provide excellent service, but the overwhelming majority of customers won't make the effort. They often evaluate you by your cover after giving you a quick look.

It's crucial to portray your company in a manner that inspires confidence and trust because of this. One strategy to level the playing field is to employ technology strategically. Not that long ago, access to business technology tools was exclusive to major organizations since it was too expensive for small enterprises. The level playing field has been achieved via cloud computing, software as a service (SaaS), and the Internet.

A well-known cartoon with the line, "On the Internet, nobody knows you're a dog," shows a dog using a computer. It was published in the New Yorker. This demonstrates how technology can help level the playing field and combat the distrust bias against small enterprises by making the tiny man seem like one of the big men.

The following are some affordable ways you may utilize

technology to help you promote your company in a wider and more professional manner. Many of these tools will not only assist you in combating the small business trust bias, but they will also enable you to operate and grow your company much more effectively.

Website: Most likely, one of the first places potential customers look you up is your website. Watch out for these indicators, which shout to prospective clients that you are insignificant or maybe unreliable: There isn't a phone number provided. Every page should have a conspicuous phone number provided at the top. An appropriate physical business address is supplied instead of a PO Box or no address at all. You may meet with clients at virtual offices and list your company address on your website, even if you work from home. There isn't a term of use or privacy policy. There are several places to find templates for them. The design is shoddy or seems cheap. Never compromise on design. Attractive, simple-to-use website templates are inexpensive and readily accessible, even if you decide to develop the website yourself.

Email address: I find it astounding how many small and even medium-sized companies promote email addresses that are provided by their ISP, Hotmail, or Gmail instead of utilizing email addresses that are hosted on their domain.

Phone number: A lot may be inferred about you from your phone number. A national and approachable vibe may be created for your company by using a national toll-free number, toll-free word, or "vanity" number. Additionally, it may aid in the memory of your phone number when it is shown in fast-moving locations like billboards or on the radio when potential customers have a brief window of time to remember it. CRM stands for customer relationship management, as was covered in earlier chapters. You may automate and handle follow-up and maintain client information with the aid of a customer relationship management (CRM) system. It's an considerably more efficient manner of handling client data than merely a spreadsheet or any ad hoc filing system.

Ticketing system: A ticketing system may assist you and your clients in keeping track of requests if you're handling customer service or questions. This may significantly reduce the amount of work that falls on you and your team to reply to emails, calls, and status updates. Additionally, it reassures the prospective client that their request can be tracked and hasn't vanished into thin air.

These are only a few of the resources available to assist you in combating the trust bias that hurts small companies. Even if you're just getting started, you can seem professional by using these tools to punch above your weight.

These tools may assist you in controlling perception, but they cannot take the place of excellent goods and services. Maintaining your marketing focus will help perception quickly turn into reality.

Absurd Promises

We are all risk-averse. I eventually understood when I saw sampling spoons at an ice cream shop. A line of people waiting to purchase ice cream forms behind them as potential customers use little plastic spoons to sample various flavors. All of this is to make sure that the ice cream flavor they ultimately decide to purchase doesn't let them down.

When a prospect is presented with an outlandish promise as part of risk reversal, you stand to lose rather than them if the product or service is a failure. This has to be more forceful than anything conventional and banal like "money back guarantee" or "satisfaction guaranteed." By having something to lose if it doesn't work out, you have an easier road to the sale, and you'll much more easily avoid warning bells going off in your prospect's head.

Here's a real-world illustration. What kinds of fears may I have while hiring an IT provider for my business? Several things instantly spring to mind:

Will they assign a less experienced technician who will fumble about for hours learning on the job, charging me a premium hourly charge for the privilege?

Will they be there for me when I need help? Will the issues they resolve keep happening?

When I ask for an explanation of the work that has been done or is required, will they confuse me with technical jargon?

For this kind of firm, a risk reversal promise would say something like this: "We guarantee that our qualified and experienced IT experts will resolve your IT issues so they don't happen again. Additionally, they will always communicate with you in simple English and answer your calls within fifteen minutes. If we fall short of

Compare that with a flimsy and imprecise promise like "satisfaction guaranteed." If you believe any of these claims, we urge that you inform us, and we'll refund back to your account twice the billable price of the consultation.

When using this strategy, you have to stay away from the general nonsense that everyone says, such as "satisfaction guaranteed," "service," "quality," and "reliability." Make sure your assurance addresses the prospect's worry or doubt about the transaction and is extremely clear.

For instance, if you own a pest treatment company, your clients would want to know that:

The vermin won't return.

The technician will not abandon their unclean home.

The chemicals won't harm their family or pets. So, your

ridiculous promise may look something like this:

Without using harmful chemicals, we promise to permanently eradicate ants from your house and leave it as neat and orderly as when we discovered it. We need you to notify us if you're not entirely satisfied with the service, and we'll reimburse double the amount you paid.

Is it hazardous to make a promise like this? Only if you continuously do poorly. There is very little danger for you if you are dedicated to providing exceptional customer service and educating your workers properly. More significantly, your prospects bear absolutely little risk, which facilitates a lot simpler close on deals. The law can even mandate that you provide guarantees on the quality of your goods and services and that you correct any shortcomings. Considering that this is probably already required by law, why not go above and beyond and include it as a feature in your marketing?

The other thing about guarantees is this: If you're a moral businessperson, you probably already provide a guarantee; you're simply not using it in your marketing. Thus, why not make it a point to discuss?

things you've already begun to do? The majority of individuals are sincere and won't take advantage of promises, particularly if they have gotten the promised service. You will come out ahead even after taking into consideration the small number of individuals who misuse them since a solid guarantee will draw in more clients than a weak and ambiguous one.

An astute businessperson would consider their company from the perspective of a scared, doubtful customer and take away any perceived hazards to make the sales process go much more smoothly. Additionally, this makes your consumers a lot stickier and less likely to fall for your rivals, who seem to be much riskier to work with.

Providing a robust and outcome-focused guarantee will

incentivize you to provide exceptional customer service. This alone guarantees that having a robust guarantee is desirable. Customers are afraid of things of their own. You may obtain a significant competitive edge over your rivals by identifying their anxieties and providing a guarantee against them in your marketing.

Cost-Management Plan

Choosing a price for your goods or services is one of the most important choices you'll make for your company. It will have an impact on every aspect of your company, including your finances and public perception of you. However, the psychology of pricing and its marketing possibilities are often overlooked.

One important component of your product's placement is its pricing. Do you suppose that the bill of materials is simply added on top of the final price to determine the pricing of a Rolls-Royce or Ferrari? Not really. The product's positioning revolves around its price.

Price becomes considerably more flexible if you present yourself as an instructor and a trusted counsel, as we covered previously in this chapter. If an unlucky situation arises when you need heart surgery, do you want the most affordable cardiac surgeon? I don't think so.

Business owners often base their pricing decisions on what their rivals charge. Setting a price that is marginally less than the industry market leader is a frequent use for this. Another popular method of setting prices is to simply add what seems like a reasonable markup to the cost price.

These are both good places to start, but you are probably losing out on a lot of money if you aren't considering the psychological effects of pricing or marketing.

Quantity of Choices

Most goods and services, regardless of sector, come in a variety of flavors or versions of their main product. Famously, Henry Ford said he could order the Model T "in any color he wants as long as it is black" from his customers.

In contrast to today's expectations of limitless options and ever-more-personalized ways to exhibit one's uniqueness, the

A matter raised by a prominent industrialist is pertinent to all entrepreneurs. How many options should we present?

Conventional thinking would have you assume that your sales would increase with the number of choices you provide. But this has been repeatedly shown to be completely untrue.

This idea is well demonstrated by well-known research conducted by a Columbia University management professor. Professor Iyengar and her study assistants put up a kiosk with jam samples at a gourmet market in California. They alternated between a variety of twenty-four jam tastes and only six kinds every several hours. Regardless of the quantity of jams available, patrons sampled two varieties of jam on average.

This is when it gets interesting. Just 40% of consumers visited the tiny assortment, while 60% of them were lured to the vast one. However, just 3% of those presented with the vast range of tastes opted to buy a jar, compared to 30% of those who had tasted the modest selection.

The end? Providing too many options may discourage purchases.

This finding's psychology is that humans are blinded by headlights, much like a deer. They are afraid to make any decision at all for fear of selecting anything less than ideal.

You'll notice that Apple often offers just two or three varieties of each of their hugely popular goods. This seems to be the ideal balance between having too few alternatives and having too many possibilities, which may lead to cognitive overload.

Along similar lines, providing a "standard" and "premium"

version of a service or product is a pricing model that I've seen work very effectively. Although the "premium" edition costs around 50% more than the "standard," it provides twice as much value.

It's crucial to ensure that you are providing much more value with the "premium" than you are with the

"standard." Because the price difference becomes pure profit for you, this method works exceptionally well in situations where the added cost of supplying the "premium" is quite minimal.

Risk Reversal with "Unlimited"

The majority of individuals are rather risk-averse. They worry about being hit with unforeseen expenses for consultation, medical bills, or data consumption.

As we've already spoken about, you significantly boost your chances of making a sale if you can take this risk away from them. Offering a set price for an "unlimited" version of your product or service is a great way to mitigate this risk.

For a certain monthly charge, an IT business may provide "unlimited" technical help; a restaurant might provide "unlimited" beverage refills; and so on. Many company owners worry that abusing an unlimited option would bankrupt them, but this is easily fixed by including terms and conditions in your contract that permit fair usage while prohibiting or limiting misuse.

There is virtually no danger involved with providing an infinite choice, particularly if you are selling something that must be used within a certain amount of time. By using the law of averages and examining your average transaction value over time, you may get a very precise estimate of the costs associated with providing an unlimited choice.

When making a purchase, people often overestimate how much they will utilize a product or service—my ab training equipment is proof of this! You may take advantage of this by providing an unlimited choice, which also eliminates the possibility of overage fees.

The extremely expensive item

A tiny portion of consumers in any market want to purchase "the best" version of a given product in its class.

Price is the metric that customers use the most often to determine what is "the best." Some customers may spend ten, twenty, or even one hundred times what other

functionally related items; for example, Rolls-Royce, private jet flights, and so on.

Even though you may not sell these expensive items every day of the week, you're losing money if you don't include them in your regular collection of products.

Even in cases where you sell a limited quantity of units, these very expensive things have the potential to account for a significant portion of your net earnings. They will also assist you in drawing in rich clients who prioritize convenience, prestige, and excellent service above pricing.

The ultra-high-cost item also has the advantage of making the other variants in your product range seem much more reasonably priced in contrast. An often-used generalization is that 10% of your clientele would spend ten times as much, and 1% would pay one hundred times as much. Make sure you're not losing money by excluding really expensive products from your product mix.

Fight the desire to reduce

There is a tremendous temptation to lower your rates in a highly competitive market. Because this technique puts pressure on your profit margins and, most significantly, your market positioning, it must be employed very carefully.

Try to avoid discounting at all costs unless you have a very explicit loss management plan in place. By offering a lower price to attract customers, a loss leader approach allows you to upsell or cross-sell additional higher-margin goods or services.

Adding value to your product is a preferable strategy over discounting. You may provide actual value to your customers at little expense by introducing peripheral services, boosting volumes, or bundling extras.

No matter what particular tactics you choose to use, it's critical to keep testing and measuring. Customers are not just motivated by analytical reasons; they are also emotional beings.

Put a strong emphasis on pricing setting across your whole marketing plan.

Before they buy, invite them to try.

I visited my neighborhood BMW dealership/service facility a while back to investigate a computer error message I was receiving. The support representative reappeared after a few minutes. The lads at the garage had made a few minor modifications. "It's all sorted," he said, using technical automotive lingo to describe the issue. To save my masculine ego from being castrated, I nodded my head knowingly while seeming to comprehend what he was saying.

"Would you like to book the car for a service?" he then asked me. The computer in the vehicle tells you when you're nearly due. Clever upsell. The service receptionist informed me that by making a reservation so far in advance, I'd be eligible for a loan car for the day. I answered, "Sure, let's book it in for mid-next month." Fantastic, I thought to myself. I wouldn't need someone to pick me up and drop me off that way. I asked to borrow the next model from my automobile.

The fact that an established client with a three-year-old automobile that has just gone out of warranty wanted to borrow and test drive the pricey following model for a whole day should have raised red flags in his sales department. This was

THE ONE-PAGE MARKETING STRATEGY

the perfect sales opportunity if there ever was one. Rather than seizing the chance, he expressed regret and informed me that the only automobile he could loan me was a few models below mine. He continues to tell me how wonderful the much less expensive model is for the next five minutes.

I wanted to rap on his forehead and say, "HELLO! Is anybody at home? HI! Or maybe I should have said, "Big mistake," channeling Julia Roberts's Pretty Woman persona. Huge. "I need to go shopping right now," he said, storming away. I couldn't believe what had just happened, so I thanked him for his time and added, "I'll see you next month."

Was the chance lost on the service clerk? Not likely. Most likely, it was more of a "this isn't my job" situation. He most likely believed

Saying something like, "Hey, I'm serving." This is a mistake that many organizations make: "He should go see someone in sales if he wants to test drive a new car." Because they divide their employees into "departments," those who are not in the sales department assume that they have nothing to do with anything sales-related. Big mistake. Big! As a company owner, you have a responsibility to communicate to all employees that sales are the foundation of the company and that everyone works in sales.

Every employee will eventually have the chance to affect a sales opportunity in either a favorable or negative way. Make it clear that taking advantage of sales opportunities is their responsibility, regardless of their main position within the company. Having an incentive program where sales are recognized independent of the status of the person they originated from is one of the finest methods to convey this message. Perhaps you will even uncover some untapped sales potential.

Making a sale to a happy, current client is the simplest. Inform every employee of the signs to watch out for, of course, but without coming off as pushy or annoying.

Granted, I may not have been prepared to purchase a new vehicle at that moment, but would have a whole day to spend with a car I was interested in have made me decide to do so? Naturally, of course! Would it have made me feel more inclined to buy? Of course!

This takes us to yet another very effective strategy that you can and need to include in your follow-up process: a test before you purchase, sometimes referred to as "the puppy dog close" or a free trial.

Imagine the following situation: you're not sure whether it's a good idea to buy a new puppy, or you're not sure if this breed is the correct match for you. The pet shop salesman promises you that you may take the puppy home with you, and if you don't like it, simply return it—no questions asked. Make sense? After bringing the puppy home, you play catch and go on walks outdoors with it and the kids. He diligently waits for you at the door at the end of the day and licks your nose in the morning. Of course, you all collapse.

enamored with the newest family member. And the dog, not the salesman, makes the sale.

It's that simple.

Please try putting this tiny guy back. I defy you!

Using this strategy may significantly increase your sales and is one of the most effective strategies to gain more business. It is built on the magic of "try before you buy." It first removes the prospect's resistance to the sale by reducing their sense of commitment to an irreversible action.

Second, it shifts the burden of proof onto the customer, returning inertia to your advantage. Finally, a sincere buyer is not likely to return a well-made item that satisfies their demands. You'll see noticeably higher conversion rates if you adopt the mentality that "everyone's in sales" and combine it with a "try before you buy" offer.

Disband Your Department of Sales Prevention

The number of companies, both big and small, that make it tough to purchase from them never fails to astound me. It's as if they have a section dedicated to preventing sales and making the purchasing process unpleasant. Save the bureaucracy, long paperwork, and rigid regulations for government agencies. It is your responsibility to facilitate clients' purchases from you.

Signs that read "We Don't Accept Amex," "Cash Only," or "$10 Minimum for Credit Cards" are the work of the department responsible for preventing transactions. These companies are probably losing significantly more in lost revenue, lost clients, and damaged goodwill than they are saving on merchant fees. To collect pennies, they are walking over dollars.

You must provide your clients with their chosen payment method—not yours. Additionally, avoid charging a premium to clients who use their chosen method of payment. Instead, include merchant costs in your base price or cover them. If your margins are so narrow that you can't afford to incorporate merchant costs into your overall price, then you have much greater concerns to overcome than simply merchant fees.

Offering a payment plan or loan for your high-ticket products is another tactic to boost your conversions, as discussed in Chapter 2. This might be the deciding factor in a sale or not. First, a lot of the time, individuals consider their monthly income and spending. Second, compared to existing money, individuals are significantly less connected to future money. Most of the present money has already been used. Conversions will skyrocket if your offer is presented in manageable, bite-sized monthly portions or as a future obligation rather than as a large lump payment.

Search for other items that could be impediments to the conversion of sales. Are you making potential clients and consumers complete pointless forms and jump through hoops?

fill out documents or follow unnecessary procedures? How may these obstacles be removed, or at the very least, greatly simplified?

Act III: The "After" Stage

CHAPTER 7: PROVIDING A WORLD-CLASS EXPERIENCE

PROVIDING A WORLD-CLASS EXPERIENCE

A tribe is a collection of individuals who are linked to a leader, to each other, and a concept. 1 Humans have been members of several tribes for thousands of years.

The ability to lead tribes of ardent fans—rather than merely customers—is one of the characteristics that sets exceptional firms apart from average ones. A tribe member is a unique kind of consumer for your company. One who actively plots your achievement and serves as a cheerleader for you. Your marketing message is amplified by your tribe members, who help it reach audiences you could never reach with paid advertising alone. These remarkable companies that go on to become tribal leaders have the following characteristics, to name a few: They never stop trying to impress their clients, which makes them devoted followers. They establish and nurture enduring bonds. They make dealing with them enjoyable and simple. They surround their goods and services with a theatrical atmosphere. They have procedures in place to ensure that they can provide a fantastic experience regularly.

We're going to examine several tactics in this chapter for converting clients into devoted followers who respect you, recommend you, and are eager to work with you again. These folks are your tribe; thus, it's critical to have plans in place for cultivating and nurturing such a following.

Once a prospect becomes a client (i.e., purchases from them), the majority of regular companies cease their marketing activities. Their ability to expand as a company is severely restricted by this kind of transactional mentality, which keeps them trapped.

On the other hand, genuinely exceptional firms see exponential growth because every new client they bring on generates income not only once but often. After all, that consumer becomes an advocate for the company.

New product introductions become simple and predictable, which is even more thrilling than that. When you have a community of devoted admirers, you don't need to hustle, promote, or persuade as much. Take a look at Apple, a pioneer in this field of advertising. They may introduce a whole new line of products, or even a whole new product category, and already have hordes of devoted customers lining up days in advance, pleading with Apple to accept their money. This is not limited to the purview of big businesses like Apple.

Small enterprises have a significant edge in this field. Small firms are more adaptable and fast to react to the requirements and comments of their customers than giant corporations, which are rigid, bogged down in red tape, have several levels of reporting, and use a diverse range of agendas. More significantly, small companies can handle client relationships on a personal level. Consumers are less likely to get lost in a sea of other consumers, and relationships that are much more intimate and tribal may be formed. Building a tribe of devoted followers is your responsibility, and you should realize that the marketing process doesn't start until a prospect becomes a paying client.

Offer them what they need while selling them what they want.

We covered the fundamentals of creating a strong offer in Chapter 2. As mentioned in that chapter, determining your target market's precise needs is the first step toward creating a strong offer. I want to delve further now. When it comes to providing your product or service, we must fulfill our consumers' needs as well as their wants.

The gap between what individuals need and what they desire

is sometimes rather wide. I'll give you an example. Suppose you work as a fitness teacher. People's lives are improved when they eat better, exercise, and maintain better health. For most individuals, the idea of improved health is too abstract, long-term, and nebulous. Rather, you must appeal to the prospect's conceit, performance, or any other particular want they may have, such as having amazing abs, a toned physique, or a terrific figure.

Therefore, you must provide them with the health benefits they need while delivering what they desire—that is, enhancements to look and functionality—because that is what you will market to them. You must comprehend requirements as well as desires. They sometimes overlap and occasionally are distinct from one another.

Does it mean that treadmills are ineffective if I've used one for a long time and haven't lost any weight? This is a ludicrous conclusion. My treadmill requires me to switch it on, run on it for a bit, sweat, and then repeat the procedure often for it to "work." Purchasing it is only the beginning. Another is to utilize it for what it was designed for. Even though it may seem apparent, persuading consumers to take the necessary actions to benefit from your product or service will be a significant portion of your struggle.

Some company owners believe that the customers must see that the product or service they have purchased produces the desired outcomes and that they have no obligation to see it through to completion. But this is

obliging many things are vying for our clients' time and attention in this fast-paced world. Our aim is for our clients to attain outcomes.

This is the last thing we want: a consumer purchasing a product or service and then not using it or implementing it appropriately is very likely to write it off as a failure. It turns out to be a one-time deal at best, or it turns out to be called a fraud at worst. A customer may treat your goods or service in the same way that they would a stupid person who claims that a treadmill is a fraud since they never used it.

However, with the availability of social media and online forums, consumers may now disseminate either good or negative comments depending on whether they have favorable or unfavorable outcomes. Injured? Perhaps, but turn-key solutions that guide clients through implementation to achieve the intended outcome will be the distinguishing feature of successful organizations.

It will often imply that you have to walk them through the process of achieving outcomes. If not, your firm is a low-margin, transaction-style commodity where pricing is your only source of competition. That's a perilous position to be in, with pricing comparisons just a click away.

It is thus your responsibility to figure out how to meet your prospects' needs while still selling them what they desire. It could be necessary to package things in a certain manner to persuade people to act and take the necessary steps to attain outcomes. To make the procedure appear less intimidating, you may need to divide it up into little, doable chunks.

Even if you have the greatest vitamin in the world, you still need to sweeten it to get the kids to take it. Giving people what they need and desire is what's meant by it.

People are drawn to leadership, and they want to be led. Leadership is shown by taking the initiative to package up the execution of your product or service, foreseeing obstacles that may arise along the route, and having answers to go beyond them. Supporting your

clients to attaining outcomes will provide significant benefits for both of you.

You two will be let down if you don't accomplish this. Recall that building a tribe of devoted followers is your ultimate aim, not simply making sales.

Make a Theater Out of Your Goods and Services

Peter Drucker is well-known for having said that marketing and innovation are a company's two core operations. When people hear the term innovation, they often picture Silicon Valley's high-tech startups, biotech businesses, or engineering organizations. It's a common question: Is it possible for a regular company selling regular things to be innovative? Yes, of course, is the response.

A prevalent misperception is that innovation must reside inside the product or service itself. It might seem like innovation has no place in your company or sector if you provide a drab or average product. It might seem that your only choice is to compete on price.

But innovation doesn't have to stop with commercial products. Innovation may be used in many different aspects of the customer experience, such as pricing, financing, packaging, delivery, support, management, and marketing. The creation of a theatrical atmosphere is one area in which enterprises fail miserably. Your clients expect more than merely to be taken care of. They're looking for entertainment. Provide people with what they want by making your goods seem theatrical.

If your firm is "unsexy" and your customers' primary concern is usually pricing, you may be a little dubious about all this talk of innovation and drama. Ultimately, is it possible for a blender maker to be innovative? or even a dining establishment? How can these mundane, everyday companies be creative? I'm happy you inquired.

Blendtec is a producer of standard blenders, the kind you might find in your average household kitchen. They've made a series of

YouTube videos titled Will It Blend? and have generated a huge buzz around viral marketing. Here, a bizarre-looking scientist uses several strange things, including golf balls iPhones, and iPads, to illustrate their invention.

Seeing the heinous devastation of my beloved Apple devices makes me want to weep, but Blendtec must be feeling pretty good about the hundreds of millions of views they've received on their YouTube channel. When you consider how little it costs to produce these films, the notoriety that they received is just amazing. Could you, in a similar manner, leverage theatricality and publicity by showing your regular product being used in novel ways?

I saw this banner on the wall of a nearby restaurant when I was in the men's restroom:

The eatery provides a pick-up and drop-off service to relieve patrons of the burden of driving when intoxicated. Customers benefit from ease, and the restaurant sells more alcohol—its highest-margin item—as a result. Everyone is successful.

These are just a few instances of typical, otherwise uninteresting companies using creative marketing strategies to market their goods. It's your turn to innovate now. You don't need to create anything novel. Model,

Innovative ideas from other industries or products may be freely borrowed or stolen.

Don't just remain a commodity that pushes competitors to just compete on price. Do something different.

Reduce Friction with Technology

I was just having dinner at one of my favorite places with my wife. The setting is amazing—right on the beach—and the staff is kind and helpful. The cuisine is also excellent. They have a wood fireplace blazing on chilly nights, which enhances the ambiance. Since we relocated to the region, which was around a year ago, we have been eating there. When I turned to pay for the food, I saw the handwritten, torn sign that said, "Sorry, our credit card machine doesn't work with PINs. Please sign instead" which was still in place next to the credit card terminal. We sincerely regret any inconvenience.

I was astounded that a fine dining establishment with so many positive aspects could have just one basic aspect so incorrect. Being a company owner, I want every aspect of my interactions with consumers to be as easy and seamless as possible, especially the part where I get paid. Not only had they not fixed this malfunctioning credit card machine for at least a year (that I am aware of), but it was also obvious that they had no plans to introduce contactless payment systems or any other new, even more, frictionless payment technology.

Over the last several years, technology has advanced at an astounding pace. Google was still a privately held, little-known business in August 2004. Facebook was still a private experiment when it opened to the public in September 2006. There was no iPhone in the middle of 2007, and the iPad was still just a rumor in the geek community in April 2010. A few short years ago, several of these technologies didn't even exist. Now, we find it hard to fathom living without them. Over thousands of years, new technology has always served the same goal, despite the exponential growth in technological progress.

To put it simply, the goal of every new technology used in your company is to reduce friction. Our goal is to make the deal as quickly and easily as possible, but

raising client contentment. We also aim to stay away from

circumstances where technology makes business more difficult than easier.

When we attempt to reason with someone who is being held back by technology, as consumers (often of major organizations), we've all had the frustrating experience of hearing their version of "Computer says 'No.'" It is our responsibility as small company owners to make sure that technology is used in ways that reduce friction rather than increase it.

The "heavy lifting" that technology does for us, such as completing intricate calculations, moving concrete blocks into position, or sifting through hundreds of periodicals to locate a cryptic literary allusion, makes our lives simpler. However, there are moments when it seems like we use technology only for its own sake. For instance, I often inquire about the goals of people's Facebook, Twitter, and website pages. I seldom ever get a clear-cut, concise response.

When the iPod first came out, there was only one method to legally add new music to it: Make your way to the nearby music shop and purchase a CD with your preferred songs. Import the contents into your computer's hard drive by inserting the CD into the computer. To ensure that all the music is copied across, synchronize the iPod and PC.

The iPod was nevertheless a great success despite this grueling procedure; however, when Apple unveiled the iTunes Store, the iPod's popularity took off, and it also served as the model for the iPhone and iPad. The friction between customers and merchants was significantly decreased by the technology that Apple offered. This also applies to Google, Amazon, contactless payment methods, and a host of other things.

Through the reduction of friction, technology allows us to do tasks that would have taken hours, days, or even years to complete without it in a fraction of the time. So, how can you lessen the friction that exists between you and your consumers using technology? Which chores are you able to make effortless and efficient? What's more, how can you make sure that technology doesn't get in the way of your customer relationships? This is how I go about doing it.

Think of each piece of technology as an employee. For what task am I employing this person? Which key performance indicators (KPIs) do they have? Consider a webpage as an example. Businesses sometimes build websites with no clear objectives, only a hazy idea or the hope that by posting an online version of their brochure, buyers will find them.

All intelligent entrepreneurs I know, on the other hand, employ technology with very clear and quantifiable objectives in mind. For example, a website may be used for selling a product or persuading prospects to opt into a marketing database. These are quantifiable items that can be measured and linked to KPIs. We can see right away whether they are functioning or not, and we terminate those that aren't while keeping up with the improvements for the functioning ones.

Reevaluating the many ways you utilize technology in your organization could be a smart idea right now. Do they lessen the turbulence? Are they carrying out their contracted duties?

Develop into a Valuable Voice for Your Tribe

It was well said by the late, great Jim Rohn, "Don't spend most of your time on the voices that don't count." To free up more time to listen to the important voices, shut out the superficial ones.

That's good advice, but part of giving your consumers a top-notch experience is giving them a voice that matters to them. In your field, you should be seen as a thought leader who is often asked for advice and comments. You do this by starting to produce content. One of the key differences between "wantrepreneurs" and successful entrepreneurs is that the former are mostly content providers, while the latter are primarily content consumers. Entrepreneurs who achieve success are often prolific content developers, going beyond simple content creation.

You need good ideas to become a useful voice, and good ideas don't usually just appear out of nowhere and stop you in your tracks. You establish the groundwork for developing your important ideas by seeking out other influential voices, such as thought leaders inside and outside of your sector, mentors, coaches, and accomplished peers.

This form of self-education is the most useful type of education I know of. But, as enticing as it may be, it's crucial to avoid allowing too many voices to enter. Many voices speaking from theory and opinion are much less important than a few speaking from experience and actual understanding. Though theories and opinions are not inherently evil, I seldom find worthwhile voices from sources that don't align with my values.

If they haven't already, the era of high-pressure sales techniques is rapidly coming to an end. Reputation is the most important asset at a time when almost all information is accessible to everyone and everyone is linked. You must switch your marketing from merely providing information and using pushy sales techniques to one that emphasizes education in the reputation economy.

Focused marketing. The purpose of education marketing is dual, as this book has covered.

Establishing oneself as an expert in your target market is the first step. Everyone is interested in hearing from a reliable source. You establish yourself as an authority and subject-matter expert in your area by producing content.

Second, it's about developing connections with your target market and going beyond just being a salesman to becoming their valued adviser. You may establish a connection with your target market by consistently providing them with informative and helpful material. After all, who would you rather purchase from—a stranger looking to make a fast sale or a reliable source that has been providing you with a lot of value?

It takes time and effort to become a voice of significance, but the effort will be worthwhile. You cannot afford to operate as a commodity or as another "me too" company in the reputation economy. How do you begin to be a valuable voice in your market? Could you launch a website? a list by mail? Is a newsletter released once a month? Typical videos on YouTube?

Any one of these actions might be the catalyst for you to establish yourself as a valuable voice in your industry. You will undoubtedly stand out from your rivals if you do this since they are still using outdated sales techniques.

Tell Them Everything That Troubles You

One evening, my spouse and I were heading home after a meal when I heard those dreaded words: "Let's stop by the supermarket." I was hoping for a pleasant, leisurely conclusion to my Saturday night. All I have to do is pick up a few items. With a sigh, I drove into the parking lot. Since I detest shopping more than anything else, I attempted my tried-and-true response, "I'll wait for you in the car." She was just picking up a few items, so I could make good use of that time by using my iPhone to finish the level I'd been stuck on and launch some angry birds. She wouldn't have it, however. At last, I found myself in the grocery store's last aisle, carrying a big shopping basket full of the now-broken promise of "just a couple of things." I saw something while my wife was preoccupied with choosing between grapefruit and coconut shampoo (which is a marketing lesson in and of itself): a masterful marketing ninja maneuver that was accomplished flawlessly. View the photo I took of it below:

Can you notice the big difference between the two bottles of shower gel on the right and the one on the left? One of the greatest uses of product packaging I've seen in a long time is the pair of bottles on the right. The bottle on the left is monotonous, secure, and almost identical to the other 100 bottles on the shelf.

Pouring a full glass of Guinness takes a while. This is due to a phenomenon known as nucleation, in which air pockets from extra bubbles permeate the beer. Although this is generally understood, at first, many customers had unfavorable opinions on how long it took to properly pour a pint of Guinness from the tap. Guinness reversed all of this in the mid-1990s by selling this drawback as a benefit of their marketing strategy. In other words, they began bragging about how hard it was to pour the ideal beer into others. They made this clear by

stating that "good things come to those who wait" and "the perfect pint takes 119.5 seconds to pour."

The lesson here is to convey to your audience the amount of work that goes into providing your product or service. Give them the specifics of how you laboriously create or manufacture your goods in your sales text and packaging. This applies similarly to whether you supply services. Tell them about your background, how you learned your talents, the safeguards you put in place, and the way you teach your employees. A crucial component of any marketing strategy should be the history of your product or service. Don't let your abilities and efforts go unappreciated. It reassures them that your product is of high caliber and substance. This is particularly crucial when making a pitch for a high-end item or service.

When you go back and look at my picture of the shower gel, you can see that the whole bottle is devoted to history. The firm name and emblem aren't even present—what a clever and excellent use of precious real space! The truth is that nobody is interested in your business name, logo, or implausible assertion that you are the industry leader. People are interested in learning how your product can benefit them, and your background is crucial to this.

There you have it, then. From being a reluctant participant in a shopping expedition, I gained insight into a novel application of a crucial marketing tenet: good things do come to those who wait.

Systems Turn You Into a Fortune, But Products Make You Money

Developing systems has always been a key area of focus for me in all of my enterprises. I became obsessed after reading Michael Gerber's book The E-Myth Revisited for the first time. The lightbulb went out in my business-related head. That's fortunate for me as well since I've excelled outside of corporate systems. One thing that helped me go from struggling and breaking into the company to doing well and exiting several enterprises effectively was the creation of processes.

Replicable business systems are the most useful ones. It will be difficult or impossible to reproduce your company if its core competency is genius or superstar ability. That's one of the reasons why investor Warren Buffett exclusively puts his money into "boring businesses"—those that are easy to comprehend, provide a reliable product, have strong management, and make a lot of money. How dull!

You won't find any speculative biotech businesses, high-risk technological firms, or unclear ideas in his portfolio. These sometimes depend on one or two celebrities, whose departure would bankrupt the business. Rather, you'll see reliable companies with well-established processes that reliably provide top-notch goods over an extended period. Systems enable common people to manage remarkable businesses.

When you have a profitable company strategy that can be

replicated, people will want to give you big bucks for it. Money will take numerous forms; however, the following are the most typical ones: Clients want to work with you due to your reliable performance. Those seeking to license your system as licensees Those who are interested in becoming franchisees An acquirer or rival seeking to acquire your company

Regardless of the kind of company you're in, there are four basic kinds of business systems that you must develop. If you can develop scalable and reproducible methods in these four areas of your firm, you're very certain to become extremely wealthy:

1. Marketing system: provide a steady stream of leads for the company.

2. Sales system: conversion, follow-up, and lead nurturing

3. Fulfillment system: the actual action you take in return for the money received from the client

4. Administration system: assistance for all other corporate operations; including accounting, reception, human resources, and so forth.

Whichever kind of business you operate, these four functions will apply to you.

Many small companies overlook their marketing and sales strategies in favor of being too preoccupied with fulfillment and administrative tasks. Ultimately, nobody is putting deadline pressure on you to increase your marketing efforts. Most concerns that seem urgent are within the purview of administration and fulfillment duties. This results in a scenario where the company, although perhaps providing good goods and services, is having trouble operating.

The issue is the fact that clients are unaware of the quality of your offerings until they purchase from you. Additionally, people won't ever purchase from you in the first place and discover how excellent you are if your marketing and sales procedures aren't working. It is a never-ending loop.

Some people depend on word-of-mouth and reputation. Even if they are fantastic, it takes a very long time to generate enough revenue from reputation alone. However, astute companies go to considerable lengths to enhance their

systems for sales and marketing. After all, money can usually be used to fix the majority of company issues.

What is a business system, then?

To put it simply, business systems begin with written policies and procedures that let your company function without your presence. These are often in the form of checklists, although audio and video instruction may also play a significant role. These documents are referred to as an operations handbook together, and they aim to compile the business's overall "know-how."

McDonald's is the poster child for business systems. This is a multi-billion-dollar, global, intricate industry that is ultimately governed by petty kids who aren't even trustworthy with their beds. How do they accomplish this? McDonald's boasts incredible business processes. Every aspect of the company is covered in its operations handbook, from recruiting and customer service to knowing just how much sauce and pickles to put on a Big Mac sandwich. I ought to be aware. I used to work there when I was a teenager. Here's a little item I discovered a few years ago when moving.

Based on my observations, many small company owners tend to disregard business systems for two main reasons.

Business systems serve as "back office" functions, which is the initial explanation. Some people think that strong business processes are dull, in contrast to the newest products you sell, your sales tactics, or other highly visible parts of your organization. Building them can be monotonous, but the amazing power they bestow upon you makes it anything but.

Perceived lack of urgency is the second primary reason why business systems are ignored. Order fulfillment, sales, and administration feel like far more crucial tasks to do when a firm is tiny or just getting started. Company systems appear like something that can wait until later, with all of these pressing matters competing for the company owner's limited time. Nevertheless, it seldom ends well, just like any other accumulation of negligence over time.

When a business owner decides to sell their enterprise and discovers, after years of arduous labor, that their company is worthless, it is a tragic circumstance. They are the business, and without them, there would be no actual company to sell. It's not so much that the business is worthless in and of itself. In situations such as these, they are unable to sell it for anything close to the value of their shares, plus maybe a negligible sum as "goodwill."

System implementation has several advantages for your company.

Here are a few of the more significant ones.

It builds a precious asset. It's good if your company generates enough cash flow to support your standard of living. However, wouldn't it be amazing if you could sell your company and get the largest payout of your life when you finally felt it was time? You can only do this if you increase the business's worth, which is only possible if the system is designed to function without you.

Utilize and expandability. Systems allow your firm to grow. You have the option of expanding your company independently into new regions or by franchising or licensing the rights to your business model. In this manner, many riches have been created.

Consistency. One of the secrets to providing a first-rate client experience is consistency. Even if their cuisine may not be to your taste, you can always count on McDonald's to provide a consistently good experience.

reduced labor expenses. You and your employees become more efficient and spend less on labor when you don't have to waste time and energy constantly creating the wheel.

The System's Power: The Capability to Fire Oneself

Allow me to pose a query to you. If you were to leave your firm behind and go abroad for six months, would it be in better or worse condition when you returned? Would there even be a business remaining for you to return to? You most likely don't have a company; rather, you are the business if you give a negative response to either of these questions. Numerous small firms, particularly those run by single proprietors or in which all partners are employed by the company, make the error of failing to consider systems for the reasons mentioned above. Ultimately, the company is tiny, and the founder or founders handle every aspect of the firm. Sadly, this kind of thinking condemns them to continue being small-scale and captive in their industry.

They often get caught in difficult circumstances. They are so busy running the company that they don't have time to work on it. Furthermore, since they haven't created established procedures and processes, they are unable to leave the company. They're therefore confined to a company that has turned into their jail. Do not misunderstand; they could be prosperous financially. Even though their company is doing well and has a solid clientele, they are nevertheless bound by the constraints of their industry.

Their business would fail if they were to go or get ill for a lengthy period. The issue is that all of the company's knowledge is trapped in a silo that is inaccessible to them. Making time to develop and record these business processes is the only way out. Fortunately, when we break this intimidating procedure down into manageable parts, it's not that bad.

Our objective is to remove YOU, the largest bottleneck in your company. There will come a moment when you need to take time off, want to pursue another business endeavor, or both, even if you don't want to leave your current position.

Hire extra personnel or even sell your firm. You'll be happy that you heeded this counsel later on.

Your duty as an entrepreneur is to be an inventor and a creator of systems. Think broad and long-term, even if you are now a one-person operation. The first step in the process is to imagine your company being 10 times larger than it is now. What roles would there be if that were the case? Would you, for instance, have someone handling the accounting, someone else handling shipping, someone else handling sales, someone handling marketing, and so forth? You understand.

It's not an issue if you now handle all or most of the duties in your small company or if you're a solo proprietor. However, if you now have to handle every position in your company, that is an issue. If you are required for everything, then you are a bottleneck, and the company will only go at your speed.

We must begin examining every position inside the company. I no longer mean a person when I refer to a position. For instance, in a small firm, the same individual may do accounting and reception. Even if one person fills both of these responsibilities, they are still distinct positions, and if the company had more employees, other people would fill these two roles. One position might be further divided in an even bigger company. For example, accounts payable and accounts receivable may be handled by different bookkeepers. Once every job in your company has been established, you may begin outlining the responsibilities of each role. For instance, what are all of the responsibilities that we want the bookkeeper to carry out? These assignments might consist of: billing clients Reconciling banks tracking down outstanding bills Inputting invoices from suppliers And so on.

After defining each role's responsibilities and listing all the positions in the company, we must now record the precise methods by which each job should be carried out.

Checklists are among the greatest instruments available for developing business processes. Checklists are simple to create, adhere to, and monitor. After you've made a list of every action carried out in your company, it's time to start recording the specifics of how each task is completed.

An abridged illustration of how to pursue outstanding debts may be like this: Run a report on accounts receivable. Send a polite reminder for any bills that are seven to thirteen days overdue. Remind the client to settle any bills that are 14–27 days past due by giving them a call. Send any bills to our debt collection agency that are past due by more than 27 days.

Do you see how we've divided the work into manageable, step-by-step segments? Granted, the sample above is quite basic and intended only as an illustration. Subtasks that are part of any of these steps—like how to run an accounts receivable report—also need to be documented.

In summary, the procedure consists of three steps:

1. List every position in your company.

2. Describe the responsibilities of each job.

Make a checklist to ensure that these activities are completed correctly.

It will now be far simpler to assign someone a step-by-step

THE ONE-PAGE MARKETING STRATEGY

procedure to do a job than to provide them with impromptu instruction and continuously supervise them to ensure they complete it correctly.

Now, expanding your company is rather simple—just hire more staff. You won't ever go back to the outdated methods of operating your company when you realize their incredible potential.

As you can see, this procedure helps you record the procedures that you currently have in place. Right now, all these procedures may be kept in your memory and available to you alone. Your firm can only be readily scaled and made to function without your direct supervision if these business processes are documented.

Crucially, this guarantees that your clients get a consistent experience. When, or rather, if, employees join or leave your company, you want to make sure that clients get the same top-notch experience. This cannot be left up to the judgment of certain employees. It must originate from the company, and the best method I am aware of for achieving this is to have established processes.

Your Ideal Client

According to a quote by Neil Armstrong, "There are only two problems to solve when going to the moon: how to get there and how to get back." The secret is to stay until you have found solutions to both issues.

When a firm is just starting, it's normal to focus a lot of energy on "how to get there," or how to succeed, but less attention is often paid to "how to get back," or the exit plan.

It's critical to prepare your exit strategy and think logically while launching a firm. Although it seems apparent, a lot of company owners wait until it's too late to consider this. How will it conclude? Who is going to be your customer? Why would they purchase your company? Will they acquire your business in exchange for your clientele, income, and intellectual property? In what way will their investment be repaid? You can better picture your ideal customer and the reasons behind their purchase if you can provide answers to some of these questions. You must consider these issues from the outset, as they will guide your company strategy and help you choose your areas of concentration. Everything you do in your business may be framed with the question, "Will this help me get to $50 million?" if your objective is to depart the company for $50 million.

Rarely will operating a firm brings in more money than selling one. Your ideal client is the person or firm that drives you out of business, and earning their satisfaction will get you the largest paycheck you've ever seen. In this manner, many riches have been created. Regretfully, a great many companies are useless and ultimately merely go down because the owner has to or wants to move on and hasn't been able to find a replacement. This is the reason it's so important to set things up so that you're being paid a lot of money instead of having to deal with the

the knowledge that, in terms of the business's worth, all of your years of labor have been for nothing.

I've sold several companies over the years, and now that I'm an angel investor, I sit on the other side and assess companies that I think would be worthwhile to invest in. I can tell you that knowing whether you have a company or are in business is one of the most crucial requirements a buyer looks for and that you must meet. There is a significant distinction. No matter how successful or excellent your firm is, if it cannot function without you, it is not a saleable asset, and you will be trapped. For this reason, business processes are quite important. It's the documented systems that allow the firm to function without your presence.

You next need to think about who will purchase your company and why. Will it be an opponent? Is someone new to the field? Is someone in a different specialty within your industry? It makes sense to structure the company with a potential purchaser in mind, and investors find this to be very appealing. It provides them with an easy way out and a way to get their money back. You should consider yourself an investor even if you don't intend to accept any new ones as the company's owner. You put on your entrepreneur hat during the day, but at night you should put on your investor hat and wonder how and when you will get your money back.

The owner-operators' most frequent response to me is, "I love what I'm doing, and I don't intend to sell." That's fantastic if your passion brings in a healthy salary; not many people get to live that way. But whether you like it or not, your situation will alter eventually. You might get disinterested, ill, want to resign, discover a better opportunity, and so on.

You want to be able to walk away with a check that has a lot of zeros on it rather than having to wind it all down and perhaps end up in debt or sell for a pittance when, not if, that time comes and you do decide it's time to sell. When the time comes for you to go, if you begin planning for it, you're

toast. It's far too late, and there's no chance you'll get the desired outcome. It is important to begin with the goal in mind. Consider your ideal client and what would entice them to send you the check that would result in your largest profit.

CHAPTER 8: INCREASING CUSTOMER LIFETIME VALUE

INCREASING CUSTOMER LIFETIME VALUE

As business owners, we often have the kill in mind. We like the taste of new blood on our tongues and consider ourselves hustlers and closers. That is what we covered in-depth in the first six chapters of this book—the sensual stuff. The new consumer walks in the door because of the "front end" offer.

I want to concentrate on the "back end" in this chapter. That's what encourages your current clients to make larger purchases. I realize that this may not seem as exciting as talking about positioning, closing tactics, or creative ways to pitch to potential clients, but I assure you that this is the part where the real money is earned.

In his famous lecture "Acres of Diamonds," Russell Conwell tells the story of Ali Hafed, a man who sold his farm, uprooted his family, and embarked on a global quest for diamonds. His quest was fruitless and finally resulted in his death. On the land he had bought from Ali Hafed, the new owner of the property found "the most magnificent diamond mine in all the history of mankind" in the meantime.

"Dig first on your property when seeking treasure" is the story's lesson. This, in my opinion, is ideal for marketing. Most companies have a valuable resource that they can tap into: their current clientele.

Though mostly unexplored, they abandon this "family" of current clients after the first few transactions and concentrate all of their marketing efforts, funds, and resources on finding new income streams.

Although acquiring new clients is a major emphasis of this book, which is understandable, there are two more methods to expand your company. Increasing revenue from current and former clients is an alternative strategy. The majority of companies, particularly those that have been in operation for some time, are sitting on a true gold mine. Gaining new consumers is significantly more difficult than increasing revenue and, more crucially, profiting from current and former clients. An often-cited statistic states that a person is 21 times more likely to purchase from a company they have previously patronized than from one they have never patronized. 1 This gives you a significant competitive edge over both your present and previous clients. Finding new and creative ways to upsell current and former clients and extend their lifetime value is where the real money is made. Let's examine five main approaches to doing this.

Increasing Costs

Raising costs is one of the most underutilized strategies for boosting a customer's lifetime value. Most companies worry that increasing prices would cause a consumer exodus or other negative reactions. It is often true that your clients are significantly less price-sensitive than you may think, even though it still has to be managed intelligently. Most clients would gladly accept price increases if you're promoting yourself appropriately, as covered in Chapter 6, and providing excellent customer service, as covered in the prior chapter. Depending on how you do business with your clients, some can go unnoticed.

For a minute, flip the roles and reflect on your past purchasing behaviors. How many times have you found yourself using your credit card without even checking the balance or making a detailed list of all the charges? In my opinion, this is often the case, particularly about lower-quality products and services. I go to my neighborhood café often, but I'm not precisely sure how much a coffee costs there. More significantly, I probably wouldn't have known if they had increased their pricing by 10% or 20%. I would just wait for the coffee to be served while swiping my payment card. However, I believe that a 10% or 20% boost to the bottom line would be important for the café owner —possibly the difference between suffering and prospering.

When was the last time you raised your pricing in real money? It could be time for a reevaluation if it has been some time. The problem is that, over time, inflation reduces the nominal value of money, so if you maintain your prices at current levels, you are decreasing them. The overall price level of goods and services rising steadily over time is called inflation. Consider how much bread or milk cost when you were a child compared to how much they do today. That's the effect of inflation. By not

If you raise your rates over an extended period, you are essentially cutting your salary.

Providing your customers with a justification for the price increase is essential to making the change acceptable to them. Tell them about the improvements in your product's quality or the higher input expenses you had to bear. Tell them about the advantages of your current service and how your next developments will benefit them. Even with your explanation, a portion of your consumers may still choose to go; they are often the lowest-value clients. Price is what will win or lose a consumer. Raising your pricing will, if done correctly, result in a larger profit than any money lost to price-sensitive churners.

Try "grandfathering" if you're worried that your current clients won't put up with a price hike. Here, the price rise only applies to new clients; current clients are "grandfathered" in at the present rate. If you do this, be sure to let your current clients know about it. By making them feel special, you may enhance their loyalty by letting them know how much of a bargain they're receiving.

Upselling

McDonald's has made hundreds of millions of dollars with the question, "Would you like fries with that?" A similar upsell technique may net you a fortune. Bundling add-ons with the main product or service being offered is known as upselling.

Robert Cialdini addresses the contrast principle in his seminal work, Influence: The Psychology of Persuasion. When two distinct items are shown consecutively and they seem more different than they are, the contrast principle is at work. For instance, you'll perceive a light item as being lighter than it is if you carry a heavy one first and then a light one. The contrast principle is at work if your neighbor is having an extremely loud party all evening. When it ends, you will find that you suddenly enjoy the silence.

About price, the same is true. The recommended add-ons seem relatively inexpensive when potential customers purchase the main "expensive" item first. Men who have gone suit shopping will understand precisely what I mean. You bring the suit you have chosen to the counter and prepare to pay the amount shown on the tag. You have only just begun your buying adventure. The salesperson is currently talking to you about your clothing needs. Normally, you could have balked at such pricey shirts, but in contrast to the price of the suit, the shirts look fairly priced. After five shirts, the sales representative praises your superb shirt selection and assists with matching ties. When you finally believe it's finished, out come the socks and belts. Your transaction value may have increased by double or triple in the end.

With upsells, you gain from two factors. First, as was previously said, is the contrast principle. Second, the prospect is far less likely to be price-sensitive to the item being linked since they were not particularly browsing for your recommended add-ons. These two elements both indicate substantially greater

margins at your expense. Although I wouldn't advise it as a

tactic, it often happens that the upsells make up the majority of the earnings while the main product has low margins. This is how consumer electronics are commonly sold: the main items have a very narrow profit margin, and the bulk of the actual profit is made from add-on accessories like cables, batteries, and extended warranties.

Saying something like, "Most customers who bought X also bought Y," is a wonderful approach to framing an upsell. This is shown to have a good effect on major online retailers such as Amazon. Individuals want to follow societal standards. By defining "normal" purchasing behaviors for them, you may appeal to their strong, innate psychological need to blend in.

Some people make the mistake of believing that once a consumer has made a purchase, they should wait to make another effort to sell it to them. There is nothing more false than this. The prospect will be much more open to alternative offers to purchase while they are in the purchasing mood and are "hot and heavy." This is your chance to include a high-profit add-on in the package. It improves the consumer's experience and raises your client's lifetime value right away.

Elevation

Ascension is the process of shifting current consumers to your higher-priced, and presumably higher-margin, goods and services. It's the internet service provider pushing the faster plan on you or the auto salesperson pushing the more advanced model. Campaigns for ascent should be an ongoing component of your marketing strategy. Very frequently, clients remain on present goods or services even when they may benefit from and afford to move up. It is the force of inertia against you.

Ascension campaigns do more for you than only increase revenue; they also help you fight inertia and keep clients from moving to a rival. Customers often look at what your rivals have to offer and hold you responsible for their bad experiences when they independently explore upgrading since your existing product or service is no longer serving their demands. All they notice is that the automobile you sold them has awful fuel efficiency or that the Internet service you offered them is excruciatingly sluggish. Even though it could have been their fault for selecting the less expensive choice three years ago, losing them due to your lack of initiative in meeting their requirements is your fault and your issue.

Having only one price choice, or one option for every category of goods or services, is equally poor. You're throwing away enormous quantities of money if you have just one choice. Each category must, at the very least, provide a "standard" and a "premium" choice. We spoke about how important it is to have a really expensive item in your product mix in Chapter 6.

Even with low unit sales, these kinds of services may account for a significant portion of your net profit. Additionally, they draw a greater number of wealthy consumers who prioritize prestige, service, and convenience over low-quality consumers, who are often price-sensitive. As was indicated in Chapter 6, as a general guideline, around 10% of your

Ten times as many consumers would pay you, and one percent of your customers would pay you a hundred times more. A colossal sum of money is wasted when there is just one choice.

Exorbitant purchases also enable you to take advantage of Cialdini's contrast principle. Your less wealthy customers will see your regular offerings as being much more affordably priced in contrast, even when they can nevertheless have many of the essential characteristics and advantages of the really expensive item.

Last but not least, expensive alternatives provide customers with a route to advancement and something to aim for.

People will always want what they cannot have, so offering very expensive goods and services can keep them interested in making purchases from you when they are in a better financial situation down the road.

Frequency

Increasing the frequency of purchases made by your clients is another effective way to raise their lifetime value. There are other methods for doing this, but these are some of my top choices.

Reminders. Individuals have hectic lifestyles. Even when it benefits them, they don't always remember to complete tasks on time. Remind them to conduct business with you again by sending them reminders by SMS, email, or postal mail. Regular reminders may be sent automatically, so let technology handle some of the laborious work for you. Some fear coming across as too demanding. Nonetheless, you are doing your clients a grave injustice if you don't market to them often enough if you provide something of value that helps them. Products and services whose benefits or usefulness eventually expire are excellent candidates for reminder letters. Ink cartridges, massages, automobile maintenance, pet vaccines, and many more services are examples. What happens if you provide a longer-term service or product, like financial planning, vehicles, or real estate, and you have no idea when the consumer is likely to make another purchase? This was discussed in Chapter 5. Maintain contact and go on using your nurturing system to establish and grow a connection. It might be as easy as sending out a newsletter or postcard every month. This keeps you in the forefront of their minds, making you the obvious option when they're ready to purchase again.

Give them a reason to return. It's about an hour's journey from our home to a specialist shoe store, where my wife was recently shopping. She received a $30 coupon for every $100 she spent when she paid for her item. After spending around $300, she received a $90 coupon. When she paid at the register, she was handed a coupon with an expiration date that was around six months away. More significantly, however, was that it was only valid the day after its issuance, so you couldn't just go back into

the shop and put it to quick use. To utilize it, you have to return on a different day. As spouses often do, she returned home and informed me about all the incredible deals she had discovered while shopping. She then said to me, "I have this $90 voucher here, and they had some shoes I think you'd like." Wasting it would be a shame. The next day, guess where I was dragged? After squandering half of my Saturday afternoon trying on shoes I didn't realize I wanted, we ended up paying an additional $200 at the cashier. We heard the wonderful news from the cashier. Since we had spent $200, we were qualified for a $60 gift card. The following event was a human psychology education well worth the extra $200. I saw my wife, who was sick of making the long trip to this far shoe shop, almost beg the cashier not to give her the $60 coupon because she didn't want to make the whole trip back and she didn't want to "waste" the voucher. Grinning, the cashier apologized, explaining that she had to distribute the certificates by business policy. The shop almost quadrupled the original transaction value with a single, straightforward strategy, yet it caused psychological suffering for customers who would otherwise refrain from making subsequent purchases. How would you promote repeat business using a strategy similar to this one? Note that this is different from discounting. This almost compelled more purchases.

Encourage recurring purchases from them with subscriptions. Certain goods and services, such as power supply, insurance, and Internet access, are ideal candidates for a subscription business model. But you have to think creatively and seize the opportunity of a change in the way non-subscription items are normally offered.

Cheap disposable razor blades were made into a subscription business by The Dollar Shave Club. That is very clever! They have not only given their consumers a great deal of value and convenience, but they also have the right to charge for their goods every month until you tell them to stop. You can now purchase monthly subscriptions for cosmetics, undergarments, fruit, socks, pet food, and much more in other product categories that have followed suit.

Every six weeks, a large, hefty bag of dog food is now routinely delivered to my home. No more going to the pet shop just to learn it's out of stock. There's no need to carry anything home after loading and unloading it from the vehicle. It's automated, so I never have to worry about it, and my supplier is probably happy with the steady flow of revenue. Would it not be possible to convert your product into a subscription service if you sell consumables of any kind?

This has the unintended consequence of turning off the customer's price-shopping radar when they purchase things via subscriptions. My dog food purchasing radar is off right now, unlike in the past, when I would have been motivated to check for discounts on the specific brand of dog food I purchase from the several pet food stores in my neighborhood. I know it is taken care of automatically every six weeks, so what's the point in searching for it? While your consumers may sometimes research the market, they won't have to decide what to buy every time they use a subscription service. If you're providing more convenience to your clients, they probably won't even notice that you're costing them more. Most people are aware that convenience comes at a cost, and they accept this.

Reactivation

If your company is like most others, you have a gold mine in the form of a database of previous clients. Previous clients have enough faith in you to bridge the gap between them and prospects. For a variety of reasons, such as a bad experience, cheaper pricing elsewhere, moving out of the region, or just plain indifference due to your failure to offer them a strong enough incentive to return, they may have ceased doing business with you.

Because so much of the work in getting prospects to know, like, and trust you has already been done, this list of prior customers is very valuable. To get them back, all you have to do now is launch a reactivation campaign. This is a terrific way to get some "fast cash" and gain some quick winnings.

The fundamentals of managing a reactivation effort are as follows:

1. First, go through your customer database and choose the names of previous clients who haven't purchased from you in a while or from whom you haven't heard. Naturally, you want to remove any unsatisfactory clients that you do not want to have back.

2. Make a compelling offer to get them to come back to you. Generally, a strong call to action combined with a gift card, voucher, or free offer works effectively.

3. Get in touch with these former clients and find out why they haven't come back. If anything went wrong, say you're sorry, and if it's acceptable, outline the steps you've taken to make amends. Make sure to follow up with them when they reactivate and begin purchasing from you to make them feel valued.

Some excellent headlines and topics for reactivation campaigns include "Have We Done Something Wrong?" and "We Miss You?" After that, you may tell them how you've observed they haven't purchased from you recently and how much you would want to.

to get them returned and express your gratitude for them. You understand.

Reactivation campaigns should ideally be unneeded, but in

THE ONE-PAGE MARKETING STRATEGY

practice, mistakes happen, competitors may outperform you, or you may just get stale in your marketing efforts. Reactivation campaigns have the power to revive a connection and greatly raise the average customer lifetime value.

The whole story is told by the numbers.

Storytelling is a huge element of what we do as marketers, and I enjoy a good narrative. But narratives tend to obscure reality when it comes to gauging and controlling your company's performance.

If you've ever seen the television program Shark Tank, you'll know exactly what I mean. If you haven't seen Shark Tank, it's a reality program where entrepreneurs try to get affluent investors, known as "sharks," to invest in their ventures in the hopes of earning their support. It always begins in the same, dependable way. The business owner presents their item or service, explains the issue it addresses, and often gives a demonstration. Typically, they inform the sharks what a fantastic investment prospect their company represents as they wrap up the presentation. The sharks will then reply with a few softball questions before, eventually, posing the question that every potential investor has in mind: "Tell us about your sales numbers." At this point, the majority of amateur entrepreneurs flinch and begin a protracted, intricate explanation of why there are either none at all or very few sales.

Several investor reports and prospectuses for businesses are excellent instances of these kinds of weasel tales. They use many pages to convey their tale. They boast about the excellent quality of their goods and services, outline their bright prospects, and support all of this with stunning graphs that show a steady growth trend. Then you get to their real figures, and it's a sea of red. I read these reports instead of the Stephen King books when I'm in the mood for some terrific fiction. They make for quite enjoyable reading!

The widely-quoted management adage, "What gets measured

gets managed," is probably familiar to you. In the game of marketing, you have to continuously track, adjust, and enhance your metrics. There's no need for a

lengthy, complex tale. All you need are the statistics since they provide the whole picture.

All your doctor needs to know about your health status are a few essential figures. Your accountant is aware of the status of your company and just requires a few critical figures. Your marketing is no different. You must be aware of your numbers and keep getting better at them. I'll show you why this is so effective in a minute, but for now, here are some important figures to be aware of:

Leads: figure out how many new leads your company receives (Chapters 4 and 5 discuss lead acquisition and lead nurturing).

Calculate your conversion rate—the proportion of leads that you turned into actual, paying clients. (In Chapter 6, we discussed sales conversion.)

Average transaction value: ascertain the mean amount of money that clients typically spend with you. (Earlier in this chapter, we examined a few methods for raising this figure.)

Find the amount of money you must earn each year to keep your doors open to determine the break-even threshold. It includes personnel, rent, utilities, and any other continuing running costs.

Normally, you would monitor each of these metrics once a month, but you might also measure them weekly or even daily, depending on how big your company is. Let's now examine an example that shows how effective it is to measure, manage, and enhance these figures.

Assume you are in charge of an internet retailer of consumer electronics. You have a nice profit margin of 50% on every item you post in your online shop, and you import the items from China. An average of 8,000 people visit your website each month, and 5% of them make a transaction. Every consumer spends $500 with you on average. Your monthly break-even mark is $90,000, which includes operational costs like staffing the warehouse, paying for website hosting, and so forth. Your monthly figures appear as follows:

Leads to 8,000

Conversion Rate: 5%

400 conversions in total.

$500 is the average transaction value.

Total Amount Received: $250,000

Gross Margin: <50%

$100,000 in total gross profit

$90,000 is the break-even point.

$10k in net profit overall

Right now, we only want to concentrate on raising three important metrics. By merely 10%, we want to increase leads, conversion rate, and average transaction value.

After improving the wording of your advertisement, you get 8,800 hits on your website, as opposed to the expected 8,000. Then, your conversion rate increases from 5% to 5.5% with an amazing risk-reversal guarantee. Lastly, on your checkout page, you have an upsell offer that boosts your average transaction value from $500 to $550. Your fixed operational expenditures of $90,000 per month and your margin both continue at 50%.

The following are the figures both before and after your marketing optimizations:

Before and following

Leads: 8,000–8,800

5.5% Conversion Rate

Conversions totaled 400,484.

$500 as the average transaction value

Revenues totaled $266,200 ($200,000).

Margin Gross: 50%–50%

Gross profit overall: $100,000 to $133,100

The break-even point is $90,000.

Net Profit in Total: $10,000–$43,100

See what's happened? Even though we only made 10% improvements to three important metrics, the bottom line saw an astounding 431% increase. The company owner in the first case was earning $120,000 a year before taxes. In the second case, his yearly salary is $517,200. Do you believe that would significantly affect his life? It would.

Of course, this is a very basic example, and for the sake of illustration, we're employing cowboy math. But it soon becomes evident just how powerful a tool marketing is for a company.

Improved purchasing power with the wholesale supplier or raising prices might result in higher gross margins and more optimizations. Perhaps with improved automation and business processes, certain running expenditures might be reduced.

The crucial takeaway is that even little improvements in your key marketing metrics over time may have a significant influence on the outcome. Large doors swing on little hinges.

You also need to monitor and measure several other important parameters. As covered in Chapter 3, the cost of acquiring new customers is a crucial indicator that shows you, on average, how much you should be spending on media to draw in and

win over a new client. This in turn assists you in determining the sort of return on investment you are receiving from that specific medium.

Your company should include a subscription or recurring component, as was covered previously in this chapter. If it hasn't already, you need to put it into practice right now. The following are some of the most important KPIs for a subscription or recurring business model that you should monitor and control:

Your overall recurring billings are represented by your monthly recurring revenue. This is the number you want to increase over time. Should it be leveling off or decreasing, you could be facing difficulty with either client acquisition or turnover.

Churn Rate: the proportion of repeat customers that cease making purchases from you or cancel their subscriptions It's fantastic to fill the bucket, but not so good if it leaks quickly.

The primary measure of interest in this chapter is customer lifetime value. Here's where the money is in raising this figure.

One of the best ways to manage your company and make sure that things are going in the right direction is to constantly monitor your key performance indicators. It keeps unpleasant shocks on the yearly or quarterly financial accounts at bay.

It is strongly recommended that you monitor these marketing indicators on a corporate dashboard together with any other important figures in your organization. A business dashboard may be as basic as a whiteboard with the pertinent data manually updated once a week or month, or it can be more complex and take the form of an internal corporate website or real-time screen. Real-time data extraction from several sources may be achieved automatically by commercial software solutions such as Geckoboard. Managing and tracking your important KPIs is made simple by this. The number of complaints you get or your customer satisfaction rating are two other indicators you could wish to display on your dashboard.

In addition to being an excellent early warning system for issues, a company dashboard may help you and your team stay inspired, driven, and responsible. Astute entrepreneurs also link rewards to meeting important targets. If the turnover rate remains below a certain level, you may take an informal approach, like taking the team out to dinner, or you could take a more formal approach, like attaching performance evaluations and bonuses to specific KPIs.

Building a high-growth firm requires daily, weekly, or monthly measurement, management, and improvement of your metrics.

Filtered Income and the Inequitable Dollar

The majority of entrepreneurs have a strong sense of purpose, and sometimes this passion overrides their consideration of the revenue's quality. I want to expose you to the idea of the uneven dollar in this part. It's crucial to your success in building a rabid fan base as opposed to a base of transactional clients. This is important to your success. Even if the nominal dollar amount of the transaction is the same, there is a big difference between a client who is merely a transaction and one who is an ardent admirer. This is because not all growth and not all income are positive. For instance, cancer develops, but not in the way you would want. Expanding a firm with the incorrect kind of income is just as deadly.

Just as our bodies need oxygen and water, so do businesses need income. It seems logical that small enterprises aren't very picky about where they get their money from since they often lack the resources to do so. They are usually in a state of "eat what you kill." You will get ill if you breathe or drink contaminated air or water. In the same vein, if you accept unsavory clients, your company will produce tainted earnings.

Otherwise, a dollar from a poisonous or subpar consumer is not the same as a dollar from a devoted one. It is essential to comprehend the unequal dollar theory. Generally speaking, there are four types of customers in your base. 2

1. The Tribe: This group of clients are ardent supporters, cheerleaders, and fans who actively work to further your

company's success. This steady income helps to grow your company. Gaining more of these kinds of clients is essential for success and hyper-growth.

2. Customers who really cannot afford you in terms of time or money are known as churners. You may have used excessively forceful sales and marketing strategies, exaggerated claims, or steep discounts to get people to sign up since they are unable to pay you. They eventually leave when they realize they're not a good match. They go, and if you have too many of them, your firm may suffer greatly from "churn flu." Since they often go back out into the marketplace and accuse you of lying or being dishonest, these kinds of clients may also damage your company's reputation.

3. In contrast to Chandlers, vampires can afford you, but you are unable to afford them. Even if their payment is the same as that of other customers, they use a vastly disproportionate quantity of resources. They often don't find it satisfying to collaborate with the groups you have established. They always need to speak with the CEO, and they often scare and coerce the CEO into frightening the staff to forward their agenda. They just drain all life from your company.

4. The Snow Leopard: This might be your greatest client, contributing significantly to your earnings and giving you hefty payments. Though very uncommon and almost hard to duplicate, they are gorgeous and lovely. This kind of customer is seen in most firms. They are often enjoyable to deal with as clients as well. The crew and company executives like spending a lot of time with them because they are so amazing. Because they are so uncommon, they don't provide an excellent growth plan, which makes them an awful investment overall.

Using the Net Promoter Score (NPS) is an additional, more formal method of client classification. NPS was developed as a way to gauge client happiness and loyalty. Customers are classified as either promoters, detractors, or passives in the NPS language. An NPS of -100 indicates that everyone is

as high as +100 (everyone is a promoter), or as low as a detractor. Positive NPS values, or those greater than zero, are regarded as desirable, and NPS values above +50 are exceptional. The Net Promoter Score is determined by analyzing the answers to a single question: "How likely are you to suggest our business, product, or service to a friend or colleague? Most often, a scale from one to 10 is used to determine the score for this response. After scoring, customers are categorized as either promoters (those who score 9 or 10), detractors (those who score 0 to 6), or passers (those who score 7 or 8). Frequently, an open-ended inquiry is asked to elicit the reasoning behind the customer's assessment. Management may then take further action based on these justifications.

You mustn't treat every customer and income stream identically, regardless of whether you classify your customers using less formal methodologies and names like Tribe, Churner, and Vampire or more official measures like the NPS combined with labels like Promoters and Detractors. Never allow someone to deceive you into believing that all income is positive.

Customers with fire issues

Firing clients? For most company owners who are scrambling to obtain new clients and businesses, it sounds like a pretty alien idea. It could also seem strange that a book devoted to marketing and customer acquisition would include a section on terminating clients. But not all money is created equal, and not all income is beneficial, as was covered in the section before this one. Occasionally, you'll reach a point when you recognize that your earnings are tainted by poisonous clients. You can't continue to let it continue since you know it's killing your company.

You're probably losing a ton of money, time, and frustration if you don't fire troublesome clients. I'm here to inform you that the customer isn't always right, despite the age-old business cliche that goes, "The customer is always right." Instead, the correct consumer is always correct. If you take this cliche in its original sense literally, you'll be living the life of a doormat in your company, putting in a lot of effort to win over or hold on to troublesome clients like churners and vampires. Unlike red wine, difficult clients don't get better with time.

Let me start with some explanation. I am not referring to clients who have a justifiable grievance. Genuinely unhappy customers are important sources of information. This kind of client is often the one who can point out areas where your company is lacking. They could even disclose something that was driving away business from you without your knowledge since disgruntled clients just stopped doing business with you instead of complaining. Resolving valid customer complaints may improve your business's stability and foster stronger relationships with your clients. Customers are significantly more likely to return business and refer you to others if they see that you are attentive to and address their legitimate complaints. They experience validation, respect, and serious consideration.

First, let's characterize the issue's clients. A certain portion of people are never content, for whatever reason. These individuals often fit the description of a detractor, vampire, or churner. They constantly complain, are unhappy, and believe that everyone is trying to take advantage of them. Even if you give them everything they want and give them your goods or services for free, they will still find something to be upset about. These individuals are like a disease that eats away at your life and your company. I advise you to release them as soon as you can.

Across all sectors and enterprises, I have consistently discovered that the most frequent complainers, time-wasters, and persistently unpaid clients are the low-value, price-sensitive ones. The most lucrative high-value clients are those who appreciate your services, pay you on schedule, and show you respect. Although it may sound paradoxical, every company I've ever been a part of has shown this to be true. I propose that you terminate these low-value, troublesome customers as part of your routine cleaning duties.

As entrepreneurs, we often fool ourselves into believing that there will always be enough net revenue left over to justify our efforts, as long as we maintain strong gross sales figures. However, you would often discover that you made very little if any, actual profit from these problematic customers if you ran a genuine profit and loss statement on them that included all the time you spent pursuing and pacifying them. When considering the poor value they provide together with the time and effort required to deal with them, most of them would probably result in a net loss.

Low-value clients should be fired for another crucial reason: in addition to draining your bank account, they are missing out on chances. Terminating troublesome clients liberates significant time and assets that may be used towards strengthening relationships and adding value to current tribe members, as well as recruiting new ones. When negative clients consume all of your time and effort, it's often the high-value,

courteous clients who have a loss of focus. Don't apply oil to the creaky wheels. Change them out.

The women in your tribe act as the stereotypical "good wife," taking care of the household and keeping everything going while the guy is off at strip clubs, searching for love everywhere except here. Your tribe consists of your loyal consumers who support and advocate for you even while you are concentrating on pleasing vampires, holding on to disgruntled customers, and devoting time and resources to snow leopards.

Putting an end to the critics allows you the time you need to spend loving your high-value tribe members more. By doing this, you can immediately enhance your lifetime value and generate healthy money, which significantly balances the cash lost due to pollution. You can also develop loyalty by doing this.

Firing troublesome clients also has the positive side effect of creating scarcity without being phony. It conveys the idea that you are highly choosy about the people you deal with and that you have a limited supply. When there's a limited quantity, people have to pay for what you ask of them.

It should be enjoyable to do business. You're missing out on one of the main advantages of owning your own company if you let problematic clients ruin the enjoyment. No amount of money can make up for being unhappy if it's no longer enjoyable. You're probably not doing it correctly if it's no longer enjoyable. Periodically examine which of your clients are the most painful to deal with in your company and provide the news they deserve. You'll experience a tremendous weight being lifted off your shoulders and find newfound energy to devote to high-value tribe members.

Better yet, you may kill two birds with one stone by referring your issue clients to your direct competition. By putting your competition in the same boat as you, you will relieve yourself of the issue.

CHAPTER 9: MANAGING AND ENCOURAGING RECOMMENDATIONS

MANAGING AND ENCOURAGING RECOMMENDATIONS

"Word of mouth" is nearly always mentioned as the main or only method of marketing that company owners depend on when I ask them how they promote themselves. I used to be shocked by this, but now I just assume it. Here, "word-of-mouth" marketing refers to the passive kind in which you rely on word-of-mouth referrals and the goodwill of your consumers to grow.

Have you noticed that this chapter isn't named "Sit and Wait for Referrals"? The phrase "Orchestrating and Stimulating Referrals" refers to it. This suggests that you need to take highly aggressive steps on your behalf to make recommendations. However, a lot of entrepreneurs believe that recommendations are beyond their control and should happen (ideally). Although passive word-of-mouth advertising is fantastic, it is a very sluggish and inconsistent method of expanding a company. Building a successful company on word-of-mouth alone might take years, even decades if everything goes according to plan. Being dependent on one source for new business is quite risky, as we saw in Chapter 3, and the danger increases when that source is out of your control.

The business equivalent of a free meal is word-of-mouth marketing. Although you enjoy it when it comes your way, is it truly something you want to depend on to feed your family and yourself? Relying only on word-of-mouth puts your company's future in the hands of others, with the hope

They consistently refer new business to you because they like you and think about you. It is quite risky to go along this route. This is the right moment to start developing a much more comprehensive referral marketing strategy if it's something you do in your firm. Instead of waiting for recommendations to come to you, you must actively plan and encourage them.

The main issue seems to be that company owners are reluctant to aggressively seek recommendations for fear of coming across as needy or desperate. They believe that requesting recommendations is tantamount to pleading or requesting a favor, and that is not the attitude I would want you to have.

It's critical to comprehend the psychology of referral marketing before delving into particular strategies. When was the last time you gave a buddy a recommendation for a restaurant or a movie? Were you doing this as a favor for the network of movie theaters or the owner of the restaurant? Not likely. Most likely, you desired the best possible experience for your buddy. It made you feel and look nice, so you made the recommendation. It's the same idea we want to apply to our referral marketing, except instead of waiting for someone to find and tell us about us, we want to direct and encourage the process. Our goal is to make it more thoughtful and trustworthy.

You can ask, and you will get

Do you recall Joe Girard, the world's best salesperson, whom we met in Chapter 5? The "Law of 250" was one of the reasons he began delivering monthly greeting cards to his customer list. Joe tallied the number of people who signed the guest book at each funeral after attending a Catholic funeral. It was roughly 250 individuals on average, he noted. Subsequently, he spoke with a guy who owned a funeral home and inquired about the typical number of people who attended his funerals. "About 250" was the man's response. On another occasion, when Joe and his spouse were at a wedding, he inquired of the caterer's owner how many people were typically present at a wedding. The response was, "About 250 from the bride's side, and another 250 from the groom's." At that point, Joe realized that the average person knows around 250 individuals in their life who are significant enough to be invited to a wedding or a funeral.

From that, he calculated that each client he worked with represented either 250 possible referrals in the event of a stellar performance or 250 adversaries in the event of a subpar performance. Instead of approaching the situation transactionally and focusing just on selling automobiles, he started fostering connections. He followed up with new clients to find out how their new automobile was doing, among other things. He would request a reference if everything was going well. If not, he would address the issue and request a referral thereafter.

This leads us to one of the finest methods for achieving your goals in life and business: just ask.

Too many individuals only sit around, hoping to be found, chosen, or mentioned. But because you're an entrepreneur, you take charge of your destiny. You don't sit around waiting for them to occur to you. Given this, asking clients for recommendations directly after delivering quality work is one of the finest strategies to get references. It's

It's astonishing how many company owners want recommendations but rarely ask for them. A simple request like "Mr. Customer, it's been such a pleasure working with you" may make a big difference. We would appreciate it if you could offer one of these gift cards—which allow the recipient to get $100 off their first consultation with us—to anybody you know who finds themselves in a similar circumstance to your own. Our ability to maintain low service costs is partly because we get a large portion of our business via recommendations from individuals just like you.

Look at what's happening here: We're stroking their egos by recognizing them. Individuals like receiving recognition. We are not requesting a favor from them; rather, we are providing them with something of value that they may provide to a member of their network. We're providing them with a benefit that will encourage them to recommend us to others.

The dependability of word-of-mouth marketing is significantly increased when we implement a strategy for generating recommendations. Furthermore, you will get recommendations from many people—not just from strangers—and it beats wishing for them.

You may be quite certain, among other things, that your clients know other individuals who are like them. Humans are drawn to those who share our preferences, passions, and life circumstances.

Another great tactic is to let them know that you anticipate receiving recommendations from them as a normal part of doing business with you throughout the sales or client onboarding process.

I promise to perform a fantastic job for you, Mr. Customer, but I also need your assistance. The majority of our new clients are recommended to us. This implies that we pass on the cost savings to you directly rather than using the money we save on advertising to bring in new business. Usually, we receive

around three recommendations for every new client. Once our collaboration is complete and you are entirely happy with the job we have completed, I would very much appreciate it if you could think of three or more additional people that we could assist.

Once again, dissecting it, we are: reassuring them that they would get excellent results. demonstrating to them the immediate advantages that they will receive—or have already received—from recommending us Setting a target for the number of recommendations (without being too demanding) will allow them to begin considering potential candidates in advance. transferring control to them by informing them that their recommendation is contingent upon our doing excellent work for them.

My definition of an entrepreneur does not include depending on the kindness of others. By making word-of-mouth marketing more dependable, you regain control over the flow of leads and lay the groundwork for a rapid expansion of your company.

Overcoming the Effect of Bystanders

Requesting recommendations is one thing, but the way you ask for them may significantly affect the caliber of recommendations you get and the possibility that you will receive them regularly.

A phenomenon known as the "bystander effect" happens when a large group of people congregate around an ongoing disaster or criminal activity and treat it much like a spectator sport.

It is assumed by those in the throng that someone else will step in, help, or call 911. As a consequence, the awful incident is made worse by the fact that no one decided to assist.

How could any good person stand by while others were in pain and do nothing? The truth is that you have probably engaged in some such behavior yourself. Have you ever driven by a vehicle accident on the interstate, slowed down to watch what was happening, and assumed someone else was helping the victims? That exemplifies the bystander effect at work. It is the result of a failure to take personal responsibility. Since you had no direct involvement in the disaster, there is a dispersion of blame.

I've gone to business networking gatherings where people have stood up to introduce themselves and said things like, "If you know someone who needs service X, then please refer them to me." The plumber then gets to his feet and says, "Please refer anybody you know who needs a quality plumber to me." The IT technician then gets to his feet and adds, "Please send them my way if you know anybody who needs help upgrading their computer system." "Someone" is who? The "someone" in question is someone else. Of course, in terms of recommendations, this is the ideal combination to cause the bystander effect. Everyone believes that someone else will handle the request for a referral. As a consequence, our pals, the IT specialist, and the plumber, get no recommendations.

Giving particular directions to certain people in a crowd is something you learn how to do in first aid training. They instruct you not to yell things like "Someone get a blanket" or "Someone call an ambulance." "Somebody" is, as we've previously established, somebody else. Rather, they train you to look someone in the eye, point at them, and give them directions. With a pointed gesture, you tell the guy wearing the green hat, "You, call an ambulance." "You, get a blanket," you say, gesturing to the lady wearing the yellow sweater.

You now have designated individuals with particular duties to perform. When a person feels accountable for their actions, the likelihood that they will be completed increases significantly.

Referrals work in the same way. Your requests for referrals need to be quite precise; doing so greatly raises the likelihood that they will be granted.

To have a deeper comprehension of the mechanisms behind referrals, it is essential to acknowledge that every referral is the result of a dialogue involving several parties. Three things need to occur during these discussions for someone to recommend you:

1. They need to realize that the topic of the discussion is you and what you do.

2. They need to consider you.

3. They have to bring you up to speed on the topic at hand and, in

the end, present you to the other person.

Therefore, if you work as a financial planner, for instance, don't just ask people to suggest you whenever you hear of someone who needs to speak to a financial planner; instead, be specific and detailed in your request.

First of all, nobody ever needs a financial planner; instead, they need help finding a solution to a particular issue that a planner may assist with. They could be getting close to retirement age, for instance, and want to be sure they'll have enough cash to live well in retirement. Thus, you

Begin by identifying a particular issue that you can resolve for the prospective client.

The next thing you need to consider is who could recommend you. As you look through your customer database, you discover that you are representing many real estate brokers. It seems logical that someone who is getting close to retirement would consider downsizing. It's possible that their kids have grown up, left home, and attended school. They now live in a home that is too large for them and requires excessive upkeep. They could be considering selling and searching for a somewhat smaller, less upkeep item to purchase.

Finally, those who are close to retirement age may be thinking about retiring or have already begun to consider retiring as a result of a local or national incident. Maybe a large corporation just shut down a branch in your area, or maybe the law changed in a way that impacts retirement benefits.

You may now be much more detailed. You might write your six real estate agent clients an email with a subject line like this: Hey Bob,

I have something that I believe would be incredibly helpful if you knew somebody who was looking to purchase or sell real estate, was approaching retirement age, and was just laid off. "The 7

Keys to Leveraging Your Redundancy Package and Ensuring a Fully Funded Retirement" is the title of a special report I put together. Please give me a call or text if you know of anybody who might use this information; I'll send you a copy of the report to distribute.

Observe what is occurring here. To begin with, you are quite clear about the sort of recommendation you want and from whom you want a referral. Secondly, you're taking advantage of a circumstance that might lead to someone needing your assistance.

Thirdly, you're not requesting a cold recommendation, which requires the referrer to get their client's contact information or have them call you. You haven't yet built trust with the prospect, which is why you don't want to do that. Sometimes they're not even ready to speak to anyone at all.

Finally, you have arranged things such that the referrer—in this example, the real estate agent—appears favorable. In addition to adding value, they are assisting their customer in resolving an issue that is probably very much on their mind.

Can you see how this recommendation is planned rather than merely hoped for passively?

If you're serious about getting recommendations, create a referral profile for each significant group or category of consumers by methodically going through your database of current clients. Who are they acquainted with? What will make people think about you again? How are you going to present them well? How are you going to support them in giving the person you want them to recommend you to value?

You can turn referral marketing from something passive you hope occurs sometimes to a conscious, systematic source of new leads once you begin constructing referral profiles and responding to these queries.

Who Became Your Clientele Prior to You?

Sometimes, as company owners, we fail to perceive ourselves in the context of our customers' purchasing patterns. We just observe how they connect with us and use that information to promote ourselves and get more and more client engagements.

Naturally, there is nothing wrong with it. However, as we begin to examine the wider picture, we might begin to find previously undiscovered benefits. It's similar to discovering $50 in a long-forgotten jacket, except far more significant and lucrative!

The purchase your consumer made from you is only one of several they will make that day.

They conducted business with someone else before their transaction with you, and they will continue to do so after you.

The transactions could or might not be connected, but one thing is for sure: before you, someone else had your consumers, and most likely they invested a significant sum of money in marketing and sales to get those customers.

You may find unrealized revenue in your company by identifying related companies that your clients interact with before choosing you. A cheap or free supply of leads may be formed by establishing a joint venture (JV) agreement with one or more of these companies that are not directly competing with you.

An accountant might be an excellent source of new clientele for lawyers. A mechanic could be a good source of leads for you if you detail cars. A veterinarian might be the perfect source of new clients for you if you sell pet food.

Although this may seem apparent, it's not always done, and when it is, it's not always done properly.

Establishing a joint venture may be challenging. Paying a commission for incoming leads or sales, or a finder's fee, is the most straightforward and apparent option.

In some sectors, it may not even be legal for company owners to accept payment for leads they provide you; therefore, some may not feel comfortable doing so. Even if it makes sense to pay for leads from "hot" known customers, there are other effective, less direct methods available.

Making a gift card or certificate for your goods or services is one fantastic tactic. Let's take an example where your company is a pet food shop called "Mike's Pet World." You might make a plan with a veterinarian in the area. Discover what kind of pet food this veterinarian suggests to his patients, then make a coupon or gift card that he may provide to prospective customers.

The best part is that there are no conflicts of interest or sales pressure—it's just pure kindness all around. The veterinarian could advise XYZ on dog food, for example. Most pet food stores carry it, but because you're a loyal client, here's a $50 gift card that you can use at Mike's Pet World, which is conveniently located nearby. They always have a sufficient supply of XYZ dog food on hand.

There is mutual benefit for all those participating. Because the vet is practically giving the consumer $50 for free, he builds a great rapport with them. The client is given an unexpected discount. In return for a $50 face value voucher (with a significantly lower wholesale cost), you, the owner of Mike's Pet World, get a new client whose lifetime worth might be enormous. A large portion of the customer's existing goodwill for their veterinarian is also passed on to you.

While a small percentage of consumers may not use a gift card or voucher, the majority do. Throwing away anything that has a monetary value tied to it seems too much like throwing away money. Assume, for the sake of argument, that your pet store's average new customer lifetime value is $5,000.

A portion of the profit from a sale that you would not have made has been given away by you. Brilliant!

Turning it around, when you've finished serving your customers, you should check who else has or wants them. This may boost the value of your service to the final consumer and turn into a fantastic supplementary source of income for you. Here are some strategies for making money off of your current clientele in this manner: Sell the leads. There's probably a competitor in a different, comparable industry who would be ready to pay a hefty sum for hot, qualified leads. Make sure you have your consumers' express consent before sharing their information, however. Exchange the leads: You may set up a two-way lead exchange arrangement with someone in a related company if you don't want to or if it's inappropriate to take money for leads. You give them your clients, and they send you theirs. The same warning that applies to lead sales applies here. Never divulge private information about your clients without their consent. Resell complementary goods and services: You may resell goods and services to your clientele by purchasing them in bulk or under a white label. This strategy has the advantage that you always have complete control over the connection and never give out your consumer information to a third party. Become an affiliate referral partner: this works similarly to the lead-selling model, but you are paid a commission on sales made by the third party you referred customers to, rather than getting paid per lead. This may be quite beneficial, particularly if you get a trailing commission on every transaction going forward. Get paid forever (or at least for a very long period) when you refer someone. Numerous individuals in various sectors, including banking, telecommunications, and insurance, have developed very successful enterprises using this concept.

Examine who came before and behind you in terms of customers, and figure out how to provide value in both situations. This might develop into a significant source of new clients and fresh money for your company.

Developing Your Identity

What constitutes a brand is a huge source of uncertainty, particularly for small firms. An Internet search yields the following wide variety of responses: It's the psychological and emotional bond you have with your clients. It's a specific kind of product sold under a certain brand by a specific corporation. The name, word, design, symbol, or any other characteristic that sets one seller's goods apart from another seller's is what makes them unique. Customers relate to a concept or picture of a certain product or service when they recognize the name, logo, tagline, or artwork of the business that created it.

These are all succinct responses. I prefer things to be basic and free of extraneous details. So, here is how I would define it: A brand is an organization's character. In fact, "personality," which is a widely accepted term, may be used in place of "brand." That makes the message clearer right away.

Consider your company like a human being. What characteristics define its personality? What is the name of it? What is worn by it? (For example, design.) How is it communicating? (Or, positioning): What are its guiding principles, and what does it represent? (For example, a brand promise.) With whom does it associate? (or the intended audience) is well recognized? For example, brand awareness

These personalities differ significantly across companies. Although Rolls-Royce and Toyota manufacture identical products in theory, they respond to the question above somewhat differently.

Some small firms get convinced that they must invest time, resources, and money in creating "brand awareness" after seeing the eye-catching advertising efforts of well-known companies like Apple, Coca-Cola, and so forth. That's putting the wagon before the horse. I would like to pose a simple question to you: which came first, brand recognition or sales? the sales, naturally. Sales are indeed influenced by brand recognition as a firm grows. Don't look at what they do as large corporations, however. Take a look at what these companies first did to grow so much.

They most definitely didn't spend a ton of money on eye-catching advertisements and building their brand when they were smaller. They hustled, made sales, and fulfilled orders. Apple and Coca-Cola wouldn't be there today, and people wouldn't even be aware of them if they hadn't focused on sales in the first place.

That's why I advise small company owners that selling is the best way to develop a brand. If a business's brand is its personality, then purchasing from you is the best method for customers to get to know that personality.

As we covered at the outset of this book, copying the marketing strategies of big companies is a grave error.

Ultimately, branding is more of an action you take after a customer has made a purchase from you than an attempt to persuade them to do so. Similar to how you get a feel for someone's personality via their interactions with you, your business's personality or brand may be inferred from this.

The goodwill you accrue that persuades customers to choose you over your rival is known as brand equity. I once heard someone define brand equity as having people choose to purchase from you over a competitor who is located on the other side of the street.

Your brand equity is what makes buyers physically or metaphorically "cross the road" to purchase from you. This may show up as recurring business, devoted customers, or even a higher price you could demand for your product or service.

Crucially, it's also essential for promoting the positive feedback loop.

Nothing, in my opinion, better demonstrates this than seeing long lines of people waiting in line for the newest Apple device, while rivals that have plenty of stock and no lines have much lower demand. This kind of brand equity arises from clients becoming ardent fans after having fantastic prior encounters. This is something that is just not buyable via "brand awareness" efforts that are full of hype. You are not required to tell your friends about Apple by anybody. You just act on it as a result of their outstanding brand equity.

Your greatest chance of replicating this as a small firm is to concentrate on sales and then develop your clientele into an ardent following. I advise small to medium-sized businesses looking to improve their branding to follow these guidelines.

Time Is Not Money

As business owners, we are compensated for the value we provide to the market, not for the time we spend. Delivering value does take time, but we are only compensated for the value we produce. We get a substantial payout if we provide the market with a great deal of value. We incur a loss if we flop. Most people aren't willing to take the risk. Get paid for time: labor for an hour; get paid for an hour is what most people desire. By all means, they want to avoid losing. While gaining anything is good, their true goal is to prevent suffering. Though the perspectives are completely different, there's nothing wrong with it. Simply put, entrepreneurs labor in the results economy, while most other individuals work in the time and effort economy.

As entrepreneurs, our financial success is a natural byproduct of adding value. We will avoid making a lot of dumb errors if our main goal is to provide value to the market. We will not be transactional or focused on making a fast profit; instead, we will serve clients with the long term in mind. Our services and goods won't be mediocre in the slightest. Significantly more long-term success may be achieved by concentrating on the cause (value) as opposed to the outcome (generating revenue).

The majority of this book has been devoted to the topic of using efficient marketing to attract, acquire, and satisfy consumers. These are the activities that help your company expand quickly and provide the greatest value. Nearly everything else is situated above.

We are paid more the more times we acquire, keep, and please customers—that is, the more times we produce value. Regretfully, a lot of entrepreneurs get sidetracked while "playing business." Playing business means engaging in ancillary tasks that don't provide much value. "Playing business" might include anything from countless pointless meetings with no actual aim or purpose to things like checking email nonstop.

You have to conduct business, not just play it. Maintaining a laser-like concentration on tasks that provide value is essential for success in the corporate world. Procrastination, interruptions, and distractions are everyday enemies that you must confront. Your firm will struggle or collapse if you let yourself get sidetracked from the value-creating tasks of acquiring, keeping, and pleasing consumers. There are always more enjoyable or important things to accomplish.

We justify playing business, but in practice, there aren't many value-building tasks that must be completed every day; marketing is a crucial one. It's critical to realize that marketing is a process rather than an event. It's something you do every day to create enormous value for your clients and develop enormous value for your company.

Everything you do in your company is impacted by your perspective on time. Entrepreneurs do not see time as money. Money has value. One of the inputs needed to provide value to the market is time. Make it a daily ritual to promote. Create your 1-page marketing strategy and, most importantly, execute the strategy. Spend time every day creating value and doing business.

Pig with lipstick

Your choice of vehicle will determine a great deal about your success. For some companies, marketing is like putting lipstick on a pig; for others, it's like adding a Ferrari to a beat-up jalopy and seeing how quickly it accelerates success.

It's important to constantly assess if your company or sector is in the dawn or sunset phase since new technology has upended long-standing businesses in recent decades or centuries. Happy moments pass quickly. Just ask brick-and-mortar booksellers, record stores, and conventional news media titans.

In 1900, one hundred thousand horses were living in New York. In 1900, there were 11,000 horse-driven taxis in London. There were also thousands of buses, requiring a daily average of twelve horses each, for a total of almost fifty thousand horses. Furthermore, an endless number of wagons, drays, and wagons were used nonstop to transport the supplies required by these towns' swiftly expanding populace. Every kind of transportation—whether for people or goods—was pulled by horses.

Trade with horses was thriving if you were in the business. Everything from sweeping up the vast volumes of horse excrement to grooming, feeding, and sheltering the ever-growing herd of horses.

Just a few short years later, internal combustion engines and electricity were developed. This resulted in new methods for relocating people and things. New York had more vehicles than horses by 1912, and the last horse-drawn streetcar in the city ceased operations in 1917.

Your company went from being the best in the world to losing more than half of its income in twelve years. Five years later, you were busted, and all of your contacts in business, expertise, and abilities were completely out of date.

Neglecting to foresee the impact of technological advancements on your industry or company and neglecting to adjust your operations properly might have disastrous consequences for your enterprise.

Digital photography was created by Kodak, but they were unable to capitalize on this early edge. They shared their meal with rival opponents. When Borders did go into the ebook space, it did so too little, too late, and ultimately at great cost.

Perhaps the man overseeing his flourishing horse company in the early 1900s laughed to himself when he saw these fancy new electric streetcars pulling up and dismissed them as a fleeting fad. After all, for thousands of years, people had relied on horses for transportation.

Then, after a few years, he could have begun to yearn for the good old days, when things were going well, while more and more of his earnings were being eaten away by new technologies. It's possible that he even became upset about what was going on and thought the government should get in. Do you see something comparable occurring today?

Numerous sectors, including manufacturing, news media, and traditional brick-and-mortar retail, are experiencing or about to experience a crisis. They are suffering greatly from modern technology, the Internet, and globalization. They bemoan and lament the current situation, push for government action, and hold out hope that the good old days will soon come back. But for them, at least, the good old days are not coming back.

Why don't they simply accept and use the new technology? Because they think like turkeys, some of them will, but not most of them.

The best-selling author of The Black Swan, Nassim Taleb, relates the tale of a turkey that a farmer feeds breakfast every morning for a thousand days. The turkey eventually learns to anticipate that every visit from the farmer will result in more delicious food. The turkey thinks that's all that can and will ever happen since it's all that has ever occurred. Indeed, on day 1,000, it reaches its highest point.

assurance. After all, it can now rest its confidence on a 1,000-day track record. What could go wrong with that kind of track record? Then, however, day 1,001 comes. Two days before Thanksgiving, the farmer arrives, but this time he isn't carrying any food. Rather, he is holding a freshly sharpened axe. The turkey rapidly realizes that its high hopes were misplaced and that the good old days aren't going to linger forever. Mr. Turkey is now deceased.

Avoid acting like a turkey, and avoid managing your company like one. In the past, a company's physical assets accounted for almost all of its worth. Things like inventory, distribution infrastructure, plant and equipment, and real estate These days, a company's client base and the number of eyes it can reach determine practically all of its worth.

Examine current events to see how important it is to get clients through successful marketing. The biggest taxi firm in the world, Uber, does not own any cars. The most popular media company in the world, Facebook, doesn't produce any content. The most valuable store, Alibaba, has no inventory. The biggest lodging company in the world, Airbnb, does not own any real estate.

Just these four corporations are valued at hundreds of billions of dollars.

Being able to predict change and adjust your strategy

appropriately will give you the biggest competitive edge. It will take guts; you will need to invest in new technologies and research as well as take risks. You should be asking yourself questions all the time, like: What kind of business do I need to be in? Which emerging technology will cause a revolution in my field? How can I work with, rather than against, the impending technological changes?

Constant strategic innovation is necessary—innovation that matters to your target audience.

One of the greatest ways to keep up with new developments in technology without sacrificing the functionality of your existing business is to take on Skunkworks initiatives. Skunkworks projects are well-known, such as the first Apple Macintosh computer. Google has even incorporated Skunkworks initiatives into their workplace culture by allowing employees to spend 20% of their time on personal projects that pique their interest. Hugely successful Google products such as Gmail, AdSense, and Google News have arisen from these Skunkworks efforts.

What financial resources are you allocating to your industry's new trends and technologies?

Day 1,001 is approaching for your company and your sector, and if you don't have a new strategy in place in time, your company can end up like the turkey.

Developing an innovative culture, foreseeing future developments in your sector, and implementing certain Skunkworks initiatives will provide your company with a significant competitive edge.

Your Shift from Entrepreneur to Marketer

Though it is widely recognized, Einstein's famous definition of insanity—"doing the same thing over and over again and expecting different results"—is seldom followed.

Every year, at the beginning, individuals set goals for themselves. Typical ones include getting out of debt, quitting smoking, and losing weight. As the clock strikes midnight on December 31st, they expect that things will miraculously go better for them. By the second or third week of the new year, they've forgotten about their resolutions and are back to their old routines and the grind.

Wishes and resolutions are closely related concepts; resolutions are essentially just objectives without any kind of action or strategy. It's likely that neither your personal nor professional life will alter if nothing changes in your daily schedule.

High-growth companies place a heavy emphasis on marketing as one of their characteristics. They implement their marketing strategy consistently and make marketing a regular part of their company's operations.

On the other hand, unsuccessful and struggling companies either completely disregard marketing or engage in sporadic, unstructured promotion. After attempting haphazard strategies once or twice, people quit if they don't see quick results. That is a certain formula for failure rather than a marketing strategy.

Some people make the mistake of thinking that just having a fantastic product or service would "get the word out there." There are many companies with top-notch goods and services in the cemeteries of shuttered enterprises. They mostly failed as a result of the people in charge not giving enough thought to marketing. Recall that until the transaction is completed, nobody can know how wonderful your goods or services are. They only know how amazing your marketing is before they make a purchase. The great marketer always comes out on top.

This is the moment to act decisively if you want your company to succeed. Now is the moment to decide to excel in marketing and go from being a business owner to becoming a marketer who runs a company. Once you make this exciting shift, you and your company will never be the same again.

This book makes it simple to create and execute your marketing strategy, which is why I think it's a breakthrough in marketing execution. It may assist you in beginning or accelerating your transition from entrepreneur to marketer.

The ultimate commercial competence is marketing. It will assist you in making your present company successful, and, more significantly, it will assist in the success of any future companies and ventures you may be engaged in. You have been the beneficiary of some really useful knowledge throughout this book. The majority of your rivals will never be aware of this information or look for it. If you act on it, it offers you a significant edge. I encourage you to take action. Knowing and not acting is the same as not knowing, as this book's introduction states. As long as you carry out your routine actions, you will continue to see the same outcomes.

Having a profitable company allows you to enjoy life as you want. You deserve business success, and it is doable for you. I want to take you on the adventure of creating a remarkable company and living an independent life.

www.ingramcontent.com/pod-product-compliance
Lightning Source LLC
Chambersburg PA
CBHW071202290526
45796CB00008B/111